Present-day notables were well known on Atlantis before that "lost continent" sank, sizzling and fuming, into the sea. Among them:

Gerald Ford as a "pacificr."

Jackie Onassis was an eminent gentleman who preserved ancient lore.

Barbara Walters was an educator who married a king's son.

Merv Griffin was a "politico" married to a lady in waiting who today is called Dinah Shore.

Richard Burton and Elizabeth Taylor were lovers, then, too, but Burton was a woman and Taylor was a man.

Fawcett Crest Books
by Ruth Montgomery:

HERE AND HEREAFTER

A WORLD BEYOND

THE WORLD BEFORE

The World Before

Ruth Montgomery

A FAWCETT CREST BOOK

Fawcett Books, Greenwich, Connecticut

THE WORLD BEFORE

THIS BOOK CONTAINS THE COMPLETE TEXT OF THE
ORIGINAL HARDCOVER EDITION.

A Fawcett Crest Book reprinted by arrangement with Coward,
McCann & Geoghegan, Inc.

ISBN: 0-449-23340-5

Printed in the United States of America

10 9 8 7 6 5 4 3 2 1

To my nieces and nephews
Marcia, Peter, Steven, Judy, and Jane

CONTENTS

Foreword

This book marks the culmination of the most ambitious project that my spirit Guides have yet undertaken.

Commencing with creation they trace the evolvement of Planet Earth from its gaseous beginnings, describe the advent of homo sapiens first in shadowy form and then in physical body, and recount his struggles with the elements, with gargantuan creatures of past ages, and with his own imperfect nature. They record man's loves, foibles, vicissitudes, and eternal reach for God, climaxing with a kaleidoscopic view of the coming decades leading into the twenty-first century and the Second Coming of Christ.

I have been extremely reluctant to undertake a project of such sweep and magnitude, and were it not that the Guides refused to take no for an answer, this book would never have been written. But their stick-to-itiveness puts my own to shame, and for the past several years, unless I had specific questions ready for them at the morning session, my spirit pen pals would invariably launch into a recital of earthly beginnings. I referred fleetingly to this fact in *Companions along the Way,* commenting that as soon as the Guides finished their dictation of material for *A World Beyond* they "began writing about creation, the advent of man on the earth, and the hierarchy of angels."

In that instance I was able to steer them away from their favorite subject by asking about previous lives that the famous medium Arthur Ford and I have shared. But after writing finis to that joint endeavor in *Companions,* they promptly reverted to creation, angels, Lemuria, and Atlantis. I groaned. I protested. I kept putting their material aside, but the Guides are incredibly persistent. They even dangled a carrot by promising to provide glimpses into the future if I would agree to write the story of a prehistoric past, "which desperately needs to be told."

Since I am only vaguely aware of the subject matter, the Guides were able to fill scores of pages with material as it came through during the automatic writing sessions each morning, material that I might otherwise have rejected. At last, reluctantly, I began sorting them into consecutive order, and soon became fired with something of their own enthusiasm as I discovered so much scientific evidence to support their startling assertions.

When the Guides would make a seemingly absurd statement about the lush tropical growth in a geographical area I know to be frigid, I would find in the *Encyclopædia Britannica* or other source-book that remnants of magnolia or fig trees have indeed been unearthed there under tons of ice, along with the bodies of warm-blooded animals that had been instantaneously frozen to death in some cataclysm of the remote past. When they described a land-mass where there is now ocean, or a sea in what is now dry land, I would invariably run across a geo-physical report providing proof for their claims. It was almost as if the Guides were arranging for such material to fall into my hands.

For instance, my spirit pen pals have been in con-flict with the scientific community by placing the advent of homo sapiens on earth from five to seven million years ago. The age assigned to Peking Man, a direct ancestor of homo sapiens, was only five hundred thousand years. But just before this manu-script went to the printers, an event occurred that pushes back the curtain of man's existence on earth three to six times that of earlier estimates. Director Richard Leakey of the National Museums of Kenya and Dr. Donald Johanson of Case Western Reserve University in Cleveland and Curator of Physical Anthropology at the Cleveland Museum of Natural History held an electrifying press conference at the National Geographic Society to disclose the dis-coveries of three-million-year-old human hands and a million-and-a-half-year-old human skull in the fossil-rich sediments of eastern Africa. Because the skull is a near-duplicate of Peking Man, Mr. Leakey said the latter's age would have to be re-evaluated. Dr. Johanson said three dozen hand and wrist bones found scattered about a hillside were capable of the kinds of movements made by humans today, and bore no evidence of the type of knuckle-walking that chimpanzees and gorillas employ. This would seem to dispel the scientific theory that man and ape descended from a common ancestor, and in fact supports the Guides' frequent assertion that man was a separate and individual creation who walked the earth far earlier than we had yet realized.

An equally timely event for this book occurred in California when Dr. Duane T. Gish, associate director of the San Diego-based Institute of Creation Research told a seminar that mounting scientific evidence supports creationism over Charles Darwin's theory of evolution. Dr. Gish, who has worked in research laboratories of Cornell University Medical School, the University of California at Berkeley, and the pharmaceutical firm of Upjohn Company, said scientific evidences are far more in line with a created universe than they are with evolution. Among his numerous examples were documented evidence of human footprints imbedded in stone underlying a Texas riverbed side-by-side with dinosaur prints—proof that such behemoths did not die out thousands of years before man's advent, as previously argued by scientists. The Guides have repeatedly asserted that these giant behemoths, during their millions of years of coexistence with homo sapiens, were one of the most terrifying problems with which early man had to cope.

In this book the Guides vividly describe three cataclysms, including a shift of the earth's axis that reportedly caused a vast continent called Lemuria to sink beneath the Pacific Ocean, simultaneously causing the extinction of dinosaurs. I scoffed at the idea that an orbiting planet like earth could survive such a catastrophic event, until I learned that modern scientists say the North and South Poles have switched positions numerous times during the past billion years. The Guides agree with Edgar Cayce that another shift will occur near the close of this century, and that we may as well accustom ourselves to the idea, since there is nothing we can do to prevent it. On the brighter side, they say this awesome event will usher in an era of peace, "since man will be confronted with enough problems of reconstruction to keep his covetous mind off others' territory."

Although still hesitant about venturing into a subject on which some Orthodox feel strongly, I was somewhat reassured to know that there is a respected tradition for this type of reporting, not only in the utterances of Edgar Cayce and other prominent psychics, but also in the Bible, in ancient Oriental documents, and in writings by James Churchward, Erich von Däniken, an increasing number of modern geologists and scientists, and even that revered Athenian, Plato.

The Guides, like Edgar Cayce, refer to the half-human beings who were the result of cohabitation between homo sapiens and other life forms as Things. This choice of words concerned my editor, Patricia Soliman, who wondered if there was a more compassionate term, and when I asked the Guides they amiably suggested "split beings," "entrapped ones," "encumbered souls," "manators," or "half-beings." But then they added, "Why not Things? They were so regarded. 'Things' best denotes them. Look up the word in your dictionary."

This had not occurred to me, but on doing so I was startled to find two definitions I had not known for "thing": "Some entity, object, or creature which is not or cannot be specifically designated or precisely described," and "a living being or creature." As usual, the Guides' knowledge had ranged far beyond my own, just as it continues to outdistance the scientific community.

The Guides say that planets, like people, are affected by zodiacal changes, and that we are now at the threshold of the Aquarian Age, a period of enlightenment when men's minds will be opened to the reality of communication between the living and the so-called dead. This will be a vastly different period from the Piscean Age of the past two thousand years, which saw the persecution of Jesus and the division of his followers into militant sects who war on each other in the name of religion. The Guides insist that the shifting of the earth's axis in this new age should be welcomed rather than feared, because on the smoldering embers of our present civilization will arise a better one cleansed of strife and class hatreds. They therefore believe it is vital to have this wide-lens view of the ancient world, "in order to put all into proper perspective, reestablishing the purposes for which man entered the earth, and providing a glimpse of the future as influenced by the past."

It is customary in a Foreword to express appreciation for those who have been most helpful in amassing the material. I should therefore like to express my thanks to Lily, the faithful Guide who has directed my automatic writing these past sixteen years, resignedly bearing with my whims and slothful ways; and to Arthur Ford, my long time friend who joined "Lily and the Group" at this typewriter after his demise in 1971. Moralistic, high-minded Lily is sometimes an irritant, impatiently pushing me toward the goal of perfection that I am too earthbound to achieve; but Arthur, with his dry wit and more understanding attitude toward my feet of clay has brought a chattier, more human dimension to these daily sessions. Readers of my previous books on psychic subjects are aware that after meditating each morning, I rest my fingers lightly on the typewriter keys, while still in that so-called Alpha state, and with eyes closed transmit what the Guides wish to type during the fifteen-minute period. Arthur Ford is invariably a part of that group effort, and Lily says of him: "He is diligent in researching whatever you need for the books, because he is interested in keeping the public informed of your communication with us."

I have long since ceased to argue with my unseen friends about whether they are real, or a figment created by my own subconscious. I used to speculate about that possibility until the day that I was marveling over a particularly luminous passage in the automatic writing, and Lily put me in my place by observing caustically: *"Were* these your thoughts?"

Certainly in this book the Guides have led me through a fantastic realm that I could not conceivably have constructed from my own beliefs or intuitions. From a cynical Washington columnist on politics and world affairs, I have therefore become a believer, at least in the writings of these stalwart friends who sign on each morning with, "Ruth, this is Lily, Art and the Group."

1

In the Beginning

Nearly every schoolchild can quote the best known verse in the Old Testament: "In the beginning God created the heaven and the earth." But where did the world come from, and what was there before the beginning?

The Guides declare that until then there was "only a void too deep for human comprehension."

Not even chaos existed, they say, because, "There was no sound, no vacuum, no stillness and no sleep. The time for awakening was a time of Deep. Yet the Force that we call God was always, for without God there is no thing, no motion, not even a nothingness."

Because of my innately curious nature, honed by

17

several decades as a newspaper writer, I prodded them to explain where this Force originated, and the Guides frankly replied:

"We are unable to answer that for this reason: until the creation of human souls there were no akashic records, not even a soul remembrance. Until God set the planets into orbit, creating motion and harmony, we souls were merely parts of the Whole, without animation or awareness. But this Force *was*. God *is*. Of that we are certain. This much we can tell you, that from out of the fastness arose a Mighty Force, an intelligence so all-knowing and all-wise that it is beyond conscious understanding. This Force began to move, and as ideas formed in the Mighty Being, they became deeds. From molecules and atoms thought-into-being by this Force came specks and particles that gradually melded together and began spinning in space, and as direction was given to these revolving masses, there gradually evolved planets which swung into predestined orbits around suns of magnetic force.

"Thus began the firmament, and as conditions became ripe on some of the planets, minute forms of life appeared, first propagating by simple fissure and gradually through more sophisticated methods such as egg and sperm and fetus. So intricate and exciting became this system of growth that the force we call God desired companionship to share his joy, and in a mighty burst he cast off trillions of sparks from his exalted Being, each spark a soul who traveled happily alongside him, exploring the world of his creativity. Many, through their worshipful devotion, became true companions to him of whom all were a part; but as each explored in his own manner some fell by the wayside, curious to know how they too might act as gods, for since they were parts of the Whole they possessed creativity and free will."

My mysterious Guides tell a weird and wonderful story about the creation of souls, the warring of angels, the habitation of the earth by various creatures, and the eventual advent of man in human form after some spirits had willfully entered the bodies of beasts, fish and fowl. Their account would seem highly fanciful were it not corroborated in many details by such eminent psychics as Edgar Cayce, the seer of Virginia Beach, Johannes Greber, a Catholic priest in Germany, and numerous others. According to the Guides, all of us began simultaneously in that original burst of sparks. No new souls have been created since, and many of them have never entered physical body. I asked if it were true that Lucifer did battle with other angels for God's kingdom, as described by Father Greber in *Communication with the Spirit World,* and they replied in the affirmative, saying:

"It was near the dawn of the age, when spirits had been created in the likeness of God, beginning as tiny sparks who gradually took the form of miniature gods. We spirits were like unto him as a toddler is like unto the parent, and equally innocent of willful wrongdoing. We were miniatures of the Creator, and adoration filled us for this Mighty Being who had given us a separate life from himself.

Then some souls began to stray away like naughty children will do, testing their own strength and acting without the directive force of God. Jealousies arose, and although all sparks began as equals, some gradually became more powerful beams than others, even as children with the same parents will vary in their aptitudes, ambitions, and abilities. Thus Lucifer became a foremost spirit, as did the Christ who because of his special devotion was nearest and dearest to the Creator. Lucifer resented this closeness, as Judas was later to do with the Disciples, for jealousy ever threatens even when there is no cause for it."

Another day, in discussing the creation of the universe, the Guides wrote: "There were many cataclysms during the period that the molten earth was gradually solidifying. At first there was gaseous material, then water, and as land emerged in solid state, rumblings, sinkings, swellings and crackings occurred. But the land finally began to flower, and the waters to attract algae and simple forms of marine life, for the energies expended by the mighty Force saw to it that all was fertile to maintain forms of life. These were already established in other planetary systems, and now the good green earth became the home of all manner of life-forms, each adapted to its own purpose. These had at first been inanimate, but as the energy entered in each began operating according to its divine pattern, the trees producing nuts, fruits, and exotic patterns against the sky, and the bushes and shrubs bearing delectable edibles or flowers, each according to its plan.

"Next came the animal kingdom, and when the souls cast off as sparks from the energy force known as God saw these wondrous happenings, they too sought to enter into the plan. At first they were content to share with God the pleasure of his experimentation with the galaxies and the various types of life evolving on the more hospitable planets. But on earth some of the creatures of sea, air, and land had gradually progressed to noble specimen, and by experimentation the souls discovered that they could enter into those bodies at will, coming and going as they pleased.

"Some of these curious souls experienced the thrill of eating berries, fruits, and nuts for a time, and then withdrew to spirit form, leaving the animals unmolested. Others so greatly enjoyed the experience of procreating, eating, and sleeping that they became entrapped, and were unable to leave the gross physical bodies. Then jealousies arose over mating principles, and greed entered into their consciousness as some found better grazing lands and fruits, or infringed on territories already staked out by other once-pure souls who through idle curiosity had also become entrapped in animal bodies.

"It was thus that the force we call God decided to form, first in thought and then in matter, a superior creature with hands and feet and sturdy upright bones, and with a mind larger in proportion to the body who could distinguish good from evil, and could control the beasts and birds and fish through superior intellect. At first all went well, but since free will had been given them, these new beings began engaging in intercourse with those tormented souls who had entered into animal bodies, and distortions of the perfect pattern for man occurred.

"Their misshapen offspring had partly human bodies with such appendages as cloven hooves, tails, horns, fins, or feathers. It was a forlorn example of willful disobedience to God, and these beings who once roamed the earth are still remembered as centaurs, unicorns, satyrs, mermaids, and nymphs. Some are depicted in the tombs of ancient Egypt and elsewhere as part-humans with horns, claws, wings, and other unnatural appendages. Even the prehistoric Sphinx near Cairo has an animal's body with the face of a man. These beings should not be regarded as mythological. They were *real!* Remember that the Original Sin was cohabiting with animals. Thus we see man gradually evolving, while often reverting to animalism. Even today occasional throwbacks are born with weird appendages carried by the genes of those misguided ones."

Granted that such cases are sometimes reported in the press, I still could not understand why the earliest humans should have sought sexual relations with beasts, birds, and fish until the Guides, in their methodical way, commenced a daily session by explaining, "In the beginning each soul was androgynous, having both negative and positive forces even as does God himself. A soul was able to dwell in a body as long as it wished, going and coming at will for thousands of years, so that there was no need for propagation. But after some became entrapped in gross bodies by engaging in intercourse with animals, it was necessary to devise a system whereby humans could procreate their own kind and thereby satisfy the aroused sexual urges. Thus a soul entering physical body was divided, each a half of the whole, and until physical death releases our souls, we ever remain lonely halves in search of fulfillment, which comes only in spirit when we are rejoined. Amelius, the first soul to occupy perfect human form, was a total whole, as were the others who knew the earth in light bodies. But with the return of Amelius as Adam, he was two parts—both Adam and Eve—and as time passed each half developed separate habits of thought and deed."

Rereading this passage after the morning session, I was surprised to note that my unseen informants had identified the first soul on earth by the same name Edgar Cayce had assigned him, except that in the Cayce readings it is spelled "Amilius." Since Cayce's utterances were given orally, and my Guides continued thereafter to spell it Amelius, I am abiding by their choice.

I was also intrigued by the Guides' assertion that Amelius returned as both Adam and Eve. Having recently read *The First Sex* by Elizabeth Gould Davis, who said women were the original leaders and were intended for that role, I asked for clarification, and they wrote, "Women were immensely important in the early days on earth, as they are today, for they are blessed with the creative force of the universe and are therefore nearer to our Creator than those who have the seed but are helpless to propagate without the womb of woman. She it is who carries the egg to be fertilized, and who gives of her own body to bring forth the temple for another soul to occupy."

We inheritors of the Judeo-Christian ethic have been primed since babyhood on the Biblical story of Adam and Eve, the serpent and the forbidden fruit, but the Guides say of this allegory: "Eve was no more a temptress than Adam. Moses (reputed author of Genesis) added that flourish to keep woman in a lowly place in the Jewish hierarchy, for the so-called Curse of Eve—menstruation and child-bearing—was the highest blessing the Creator could bestow on his beloved souls: the power of cocreating life with himself. Small enough price to pay for such a signal honor, for did not God give something of himself to create the souls of all of us? And since each of us returns to earth again and again, some-times as man and other times as woman, the honor is not reserved for any one class of souls, but for all of us to have that achievement of coproducing life."

Another day the Guides continued their disserta-tion on the so-called war between the sexes, writing, "Remember that women were as active as men in producing the wonders of an ancient age, for there was no differentiation between sexes and each was half of the whole. God himself is totally whole, being neither male nor female, and the only reason Jesus spoke of God as 'Our Father' was to conform to the customs of the times. In the Semitic race man was the head of the household, and women were often treated like chattel; yet look at the wondrous women depicted in the Old and New Testaments! The Hebrew males were chauvinists, many of them bigoted, narrow, and full of self-aggrandizement. Too bad, but eventually the pendulum will swing back and woman will again take her rightful place on an equality with man. Remember that each of us has at times been man and woman, so we are not casting a stone at any particular group of souls."

The Garden of Eden, according to the Guides, was a figurative place located on no particular landmass, as the entire earth in the Adam-Eve days was green and verdant, without ugliness or barrenness. The snake was merely a symbol for the *kundalini* (the creative power which lies coiled like a serpent at the base of the spine, until awakened) and the forbidden fruit was the opening of the seven *chakras* (the psychic centers, or ductless glands) too suddenly, with the stress on the gonads (the earthly center) rather than on the pineal (the Christ center) and the pituitary (the master gland, or God force).

The beginnings of man on earth represented an achievement of monumental proportions, the Guides say, for not only was he superior in mind and body to all other creatures, but was inhabited by the spirit of God, and having been given free will he was able to arrive at decisions after reasoning— something totally alien to the animal kingdom. He was permitted to choose his own course, to love and even to hate, for as a segment of God he could create thought patterns and project them into reality. "Truly a marvelous advancement over the herd instinct of those created before him! Thus man became individual, yet he was a part of the wondrous Whole, and to admit of dislike or contempt for another human being is to hate oneself and the Creator. Each of us is a part of the original Whole and will ever be fragmented until the day comes when all are reunited in God."

The Guides for several years have been dictating material for a book about Creation, but I could not bring myself to begin work on the manuscript. Lily, Arthur and the Group seemed puzzled by my unaccustomed lack of industry, until one morning before the regular session I typed this message to them: "I feel that we do not have enough *original* material, because what you have told me is similar to that which Edgar Cayce and other physics have provided."

Calmly and dispassionately, the Guides replied, "Now that we understand your reasoning, let us say that all sources with access to the akashic records will naturally report the same truths. Edgar Cayce correctly reported that Amelius was the first of the angels who came in human form as a thought pattern, and after he proved able to function in the earth, others came. As Cayce and we have told you, some souls defiled the perfect plan by procreation with animals, so that monstrosities were produced, and this continued for many millenia.

"But remember this: after human souls were separated into male and female so that they could produce their own kind, God imposed Divine laws making it impossible for human beings to produce offspring as a result of cohabitation with any other species. Five races of humans simultaneously entered the earth, each developing different pigmentation to cope with the varying rays of the sun, and color to harmonize with his environment. Amelius returned as Adam-Eve, hoping to demonstrate that spirit could live in physical body without greed or envy, reigning over the animal and mineral kingdoms in perfect harmony.

"In this way the earth was peopled. These spirits in human body were able to communicate with each other by thought, or what you nowadays call ESP; and they were also able to free themselves of earthly forces in order to create giant objects and seemingly lift them from one place to another. Actually they were disassembling and reassembling the atoms and molecules, and through this once simple method we have the giant heads on Easter Island, the great pyramid of Egypt, and many other remnants of a far greater civilization than we know today."

We shall hear considerably more about Easter Island and pyramids in subsequent chapters.

2

Man in the Earth

All psychic sources agree that the lost continent of Mu, or Lemuria, was the cradle of civilization. The Guides describe it as a mighty landmass extending from the northern reaches of California to the tip of Peru, and encompassing a vast Pacific area of which Hawaii, Tahiti, Polynesia, and Easter Island are remnants. Western California, then a part of Lemuria's seaboard, was separated from North America by ocean, as the Great Salt Lake in Utah still mutely attests. The Mississippi basin was the west coast of our present United States, but with the sinking of Lemuria and the upheaval of land creating the Rocky and Appalachian mountain chains, the Mississippi flowed into the Great Lakes for a time, before another cataclysm again altered the topography.

The Guides place the date for the advent of homo sapiens on earth some five to seven million years ago, and point out that the grotesque half-human forms had existed for millions of years previously. Modern science is beginning to corroborate this antiquity of man, although one can imagine the cry of outrage there would have been in the late eighteenth century if this heretical statement had been made then. The second edition of the *Encyclopædia Britannica* (1777-83) categorically states: "Concerning the number of years which have elapsed since the creation of the world, there have been many disputes. The compilers of the Universal History determine it to have taken place in the year 4305 B.C. so that, according to them, the world is now in the 6096th year of its age. Others think it was created only 4000 years B.C. so that it hath not yet attained its 6000th year. Be this as it will, however, the whole account of the creation rests on the truth of the Mosaic history; and which we must of necessity accept, because we can find no other which does not either abound with the grossest absurdities, or lead us into absolute darkness. The Chinese and Egyptian pretensions to antiquity are so absurd and ridiculous that the bare reading must be a sufficient confutation of them to every reasonable person."

The Guides will have much to say about the great antiquity of China and Egypt later in this book, but meanwhile, in their inimitable narrative style, they declared, "Now on Mu there lived a holy one who shed light on the path for others. The archetype of the human race, his name was Amelius, and he was so light in body that he could appear almost simultaneously in any part of the earth. This was the first appearance of the Christ Spirit, and as others came to inhabit light human form, he taught them how to project thought forms into reality, even as we today first form a thought pattern before creating an invention; and how to transport heavy objects through the dissolution and reassemblage of atoms. Amelius was a pure projection of the Creator. But when the fallen Lucifer who sought to put self before God also joined the physical forces of earth, evil entered and turmoil arose in many quarters. Some of these Godlike souls were enticed to cohabit with those who had previously entered animal bodies, and they produced offspring who were desecrations of the Perfect Plan."

According to Lily, Art and the Group, many of these early men were at least twelve feet tall, and the animals, fish and fowl with whom they engaged in intercourse produced large, misshapen offspring, some of whom were nevertheless so talented that they later came to be worshiped in Greek and Roman mythology.

"God grieved at this desecration of his perfect pattern," the Guides wrote, "and for a time turned away from the earth while overseeing the development of other parts of the galaxy. But at last the torment of the souls entrapped in animal-like bodies attracted his singular attention, so that in his mercy he created man like unto himself, yet lacking his totality."

I am not a student of the Bible, but some six months after the Guides set forth this astounding assertion, I chanced across the sixth chapter of Genesis, which in verses four through seven declares: "There were giants in the earth in those days; and also after that, when the sons of God came in unto the daughters of men, and they bare children to them, the same became mighty men which were of old, men of renown. And God saw that the wickedness of man was great in the earth, and that every imagination of the thoughts of his heart was only evil continually. And it repented the Lord that he had made man on the earth, and it grieved him at his heart. And the Lord said, I will destroy man whom I have created from the face of the earth, both man, and beast, and the creeping thing, and the fowls of the air; for it repenteth me that I have made them." Verse twelve adds: "And God looked upon the earth, and, behold, it was corrupt; for all flesh had corrupted his way upon the earth."

These Biblical passages seem to suggest that the "sons of God" had been pure creations, whereas the "daughters of men" may have been produced through a defiled kind of cohabitation. Perhaps with animals? Otherwise, why would it offend God that humans utilized his divine plan for reproduction of the human species? And why would he regret that he had made beasts and fowl as well as men, unless they too had been corrupted?

One day the Guides began their daily typing session by declaring, "We will tell you something of those days when Amelius walked the earth in light form, when man was not solidly in the earth magnetism, and thus was not affected by its pull of gravity. Amelius was androgynous, as we have said, with both positive and negative forces, a perfect model for present man except that he was unable to eat, digest, or multiply. These abilities were to come later when homo sapiens was sexually divided and drew force from the earth rather than the air. Those early immortals who knew no physical death remained always at the prime of life, as there was then no aging process brought on through earth's environ to physical man, and no death.

"They were simultaneously wherever they wished to be, much as a television image is now seen in any part of the globe with proper reception channels. They were on Atlantis and Lemuria, in America and Asia and Africa, and as they dispersed throughout these areas, they sought to reassure those inhabiting grotesque bodies that escape existed if they would forsake sex with animals, cease multiplying the Original Sin by producing young, and stop partaking of animal flesh which bound them to the earth's environs. They also taught these unfortunate offspring how to dissolve atoms and lift giant objects from one sphere to another, and some of these misshapen ones produced magnificent works of art under their supervision."

But the Guides say that despite their opportunity to leave animal-like bodies in which they had become entrapped, many of the souls continued to lust after others, so that there was danger of assimilating all manner of animal, fish, and fowl into one incongruous mass.

"Thus God introduced the divine law that like produces like, so that matings between dissimilar ones became impossible," they said. "Man could no longer lie down with beasts, birds or fish and produce young with weird appendages. Although some continued to try, they could not reproduce, just as a mule today which is a hybrid of mare and donkey cannot reproduce itself. It was over four million years ago that the first Adams and Eves, as separated sexes, began populating the earth, and the Golden Age on Mu was so spiritual that one can scarcely conceive of it today: a veritable Garden of Eden with undulating plains, unsullied brooks, and rivers with splashing cascades that flowed over rocks and rills toward the salty ocean which then covered the western United States. Life on Mu was fruitful and exalting for those who kept themselves free of the animal-like world of Original Sin. Leaders naturally emerged, as they had done in spirit and as they will do unto the end of the earth, for some are natural leaders with more vivid imagination and more marked idealism than others who have lazily refused to develop their innate talents."

At this point I asked a question that had been troubling me for some time. Why in one reading did the great psychic Edgar Cayce place the Garden of Eden in Atlantis, and another time in Caucasia or Carpathia, while the Guides spoke principally of

Mu? The Guides responded: "In the beginning of human life there were five Gardens of Eden, if you choose to call them that, and five races of man. Thus there is no conflict between what Cayce said at different times, because 'Garden of Eden' is a mere figure of speech representing harmony between man and God, a harmony that was disrupted by cohabitation with animal life."

Shortly after receiving this material from the Guides, I attended a seminar conducted by Shirley Winston, a lecturer with the Association for Research and Enlightenment who has a rare ability to understand and interpret the readings of Edgar Cayce, whose obtuse terms are often incomprehensible to me. Inasmuch as the Guides had flatly stated that Amelius appeared first on Mu, I was surprised to hear her say that Cayce while in trance state had placed Amelius first on Atlantis.

At the earliest opportunity I therefore asked the Guides to explain this discrepancy, and they replied: "Edgar Cayce had little interest in reading the akashic records of Mu, since he himself began physical life as an Atlantean, as did nearly all those for whom he gave life readings. Amelius, as we have stressed, could be anywhere and everywhere. Mu was the first of the land areas to be occupied by Amelius and other shadow-like souls, but they were also on Atlantis and every other part of the globe, and when God later separated each soul into two sexes for procreation and companionship, human beings appeared simultaneously in the five existent geographical areas. Amelius and the other prototypes of the human race came directly from spirit, almost like a thought projection, and as yet had cast no blemish on their akashic records."

I asked how they communicated with one another, and they wrote, "These souls brought with them a knowledge of language comprised of thought projection, and the grammar they rapidly put into use has been a wonder of the ages. Sound was there to be tested with physical lips, and each thought symbol was given a distinctive sound, so that they achieved in a brief period the most perfect language of communication ever known, but sadly debased in the years since man lost his constant awareness of the spirit realm. In times past these humans who developed the powers of speech and expression knew the mysteries of direct communication with those not yet in physical form; and so advanced was the early population that none was born without this living awareness of God and man, the equality of all beings in the eyes of God, and the necessity each for the other to comprise a total whole. The thoughts previously projected through vibrations now were translated into sounds, and words came into being almost as if they sprang full grown from the head of Zeus. The structure of grammar and the vocabulary were well nigh perfect, for in the translation from thought to actual human sounds, little was lost. It was only later that language became degraded, as it continued to be used in widely separated areas by descendants of the original souls who altered the pronunciation, created new words for different objects, and introduced slovenly short-cuts in grammatical construction."

If true, this could explain a poser that has baffled today's scholars. Until recently scientists assumed that the human race has been gradually evolving from original savagery. But if earliest man was a barbarous cave dweller, and his progress has been steadily upward in the scale of civilization, how can we explain the existence of ancient languages with grammatical construction far more sophisticated than that in use today? Colonel James Churchward, a nineteenth-century British army officer who spent many years in Tibet, India, Central and North America translating obscure tablets and writings dating from prehistoric times, makes a persuasive case for his thesis that all languages descend from one tongue used in "the Motherland of man on Mu." In his fascinating series of books on Mu, now widely available in paperback a half-century later, Churchward reproduces many alphabetical symbols in various ancient tongues which are identical, and which indicate a common origin on the lost continent of Lemuria. Genesis also says the whole earth was of one language and one speech.

The Guides claim that the early humans multiplied rapidly, "for in those times procreation was effortless and natural, and many women bore dozens of children during their long life-spans." They say their attunement to creative forces was so perfect that no illness or disease existed, so that they could remain in physical body as long as they chose. "But as they became more earthbound and heavier in substance, accidents naturally occurred, since the souls were not accustomed to protecting themselves from barriers through which they previously, as light bodies, had effortlessly passed. Thus some returned to spirit for no reason other than that they had inadvertently destroyed their ability to sustain life in the physical body they had entered. But as rapidly as they chose, they could return to other bodies as babies."

Interestingly, the Book of Genesis assigns a lifespan of nearly a thousand years to early patriarchs, but states that after God expressed his displeasure with the human and animal species, he reduced the term to 120 years.

Speaking of those prehistoric times, the Guides wrote: "The earth was beginning to cool off from a molten mass, and all was fresh and unspoiled. But throughout aeons of time many cataclysms occurred as the earth continued to cool, bubbling up here and there, sinking and shifting and contracting so that surfaces were frequently changing, and what had been water became dry land, or vice versa. Thus as a sculptor changes the appearance of a ball of clay by pressing here and pushing there to form a face or figure, so did the mightiest Sculptor change the face of the earth, creating mountains and declivities by universal laws."

Colonel Churchward in his Mu books offers an explanation for these changes by attributing them to vast gas pockets which explode beneath the surface of an ever-changing earth. The Guides say that near the end of this century another such cataclysm will occur, with masses of earth disappearing into the sea, dry land emerging from the oceans, frigid areas becoming tropical, and torrid zones cool. Some geologists, asserting that such a shift of the axis has occurred numerous times in ages past, cite as partial proof the tropical plants and the remains of warm-blooded animals and dinosaurs found imbedded in tons of ice in polar regions. Dr. Frank Hibben, a professor of archaeology at the University of New Mexico, estimates in *The Lost Americans* that forty million animals froze to death almost instantly in the last such polar shift.

According to the Guides, forces have long been set in motion for another such cataclysm, but those who fear the calamity should remember that life on the physical plane is tenuous at best. Our goal is the achievement of perfection, so that man need not return to physical form. Devotion to earthly possessions is a barrier to soul advancement, they say, whereas in the spirit state possessions mean nothing because anything desired or needed is instantly produced through thought forms, and as easily erased. Those who fear physical annihilation should bear in mind that if their possessions are lost in earthly upheavals they are easily reproduced through mental pictures in spirit, and although the physical body itself is lost, the soul continues through all eternity.

The Guides contend that the sole reason for creating five separate races was to help man cope with climatic conditions, and that in today's jet age of travel and shifting population, color should not be a barrier to intermarriage. They say Blacks acquired their hue for protection from the tropical sun and to provide camouflage in the darkness of African jungles. Whites appeared in colder regions of winter snows, where little pigmentation was required for protection from the slanting rays of the sun. Brown was assigned for those in the semitropical areas of the windswept Pacific, Red to harmonize with the red clay of Atlantis and America, and Yellow for the Orient with its sun-kissed topography and yellowish soil.

"Thus for every race there was an Adam, or whatever name one wishes to call him," the Guides aver, "and each had an Eve who was the symbol for creativity of perfect human beings without animalistic appendages."

My mysterious pen pals agree with Edgar Cayce that Amelius returned as Adam and Eve, and that both were to come again several million years later as Jesus and Mary. I had grave misgivings about the early date assigned by the Guides to the momentous appearance of homo sapiens, until on October 31, 1975, I read an Associated Press account from Washington, D.C., which began: "The oldest known fossil remains of man's ancient ancestors have been discovered in a dry river bed in East Africa, scientists announced yesterday. The fossilized teeth and jaw bones of eleven individuals have been accurately dated by radioactive isotope techniques at between 3.35 million and 3.75 million years old, they said. 'These are good firm dates. They are now the earliest, firmly dated hominid remains anywhere in the world,' archae-ologist Mary Leakey told a news conference. Hom-inid is a general term for man's ancestors."

In the April 14, 1975, issue of *Time* magazine, I found an article about Peking man, which reads: "Study of his 500,000 year old remains using new methods might resolve a current controversy about evolution. Until Peking Man was discovered, most researchers assumed that the human family tree first took root in Africa. The existence of such a highly evolved individual in China suggests that there is more than one tree."

My Guides and Mr. Cayce had been saying for a long time that there were five different family trees.

3

Land of Lemuria

At the dawn of civilization on Lemuria, the Guides say that every variety of tree and plant existed "in pairs," so that living was virtually effortless. But as the population increased "homo sapiens had to bestir himself to provide more food, and also more shade, as there were then no mountains to cast long shadows." Previously nomadic, man now began to gather seeds for sowing, and to plant acorns, pits, and nuts. This was the beginning of husbandry, and "the art of agriculture was an achievement as tremendous then as moon travel is today."

Many Lemurians were fishermen who developed great talent for seafaring. Initially they inhabited the seacoast areas before moving inland, "and they had sheep and other domesticated animals which they at first regarded as brothers, but later killed for food as the population became more dense." Although most of the people were exceedingly tall by today's standards, the Guides say that "others in those early experimental times were tinier than our midgets, and all loved to sing and dance to rhythms of the flute and drum."

I asked about the religion on Mu, and the Guides responded: "The early Lemurians were so spiritual that they still walked with God in the sense that he sent them sensory instructions that all could comprehend. But gradually they became more bound to the earth, so that their bodies grew denser and their all-seeing third eye began to cloud over. Some who lived frugally, ate sparingly, and continued to give thanks to the Creator remained able to communicate with him, and as time passed these souls shut themselves off from the pleasures of the earthlings in order to retain their spirit likeness to God. To the others they gave instructions which were so obviously pure and right that the people shared their harvests with them. Thus the first priestly caste was born.

"These spiritual beings still retained the ability to disassemble atoms and move great stones. They tried to keep the language pure by interpreting the symbols to little children, teaching them to feel the rightness of each sound as it emerged from their lips. These children were new souls in the sense that they had not previously lived in physical body, although they were as old in point of creation as any other, and many were the spirits eager to come into the earth and try their wings, so to speak, in the great experiment."

Mention of "disassembling atoms" prompted me to ask about the origin of the huge heads on Easter Island. The Guides replied that these mysterious monoliths still mark the site of a great ceremonial center on Mu, to which Lemurians came from all parts of the continent. "These great faces with different expressions represented subgods, each having his own specialty over which to rule, and they faced out toward every corner of the world. They were raised in earliest times when man had not yet become completely entrapped by gravity and thus were easily fashioned as a manifestation of the divine spirit."

Another day the Guides offered an anecdote to enliven their discussion of the monoliths which have baffled modern man, writing, "In the time of the priestly caste on Mu there were those who resented their predominance and sought to undermine their authority. These were Lucifer types who wanted to assert their own supremacy, so they delivered a challenge to priests of the temple that was situated on the present site of Easter Island: those who could transport a giant head from one space to another would receive gifts of adornments and would take precedence over others. These wily challengers had perfected a way to move large objects through a kind of mind control during which men, under light hypnosis, were able in unison to lift tremendous weights. A vast throng assembled, and at the appointed time the challengers marched forward, said their mumbo jumbo, and with one accord set their shoulders beneath the chin of one of the stone heads that had been created thousands of years earlier. Through this form of mind control they were actually able to lift it a few inches, but then these dozens and dozens of men who had marched forward so confidently fell back in total exhaustion. Now it was the turn of the priests, and utilizing the virtually lost art of disassembling atoms, they chanted in unison, raised their eyes to the heavens, and with a gesture of the hands, caused the giant head to vanish. 'Give us back our head,' shouted the fearful crowd. 'As you will,' said the high priest, and there on a different knoll the giant head appeared. Thus were the challengers put to shame, and the priests thereafter continued their spiritual works unmolested."

The Guides say that in those times souls sometimes visited from other planetary systems, and although their appearance while in their own realm was totally different, they were able when on earth to assume the guise of homo sapiens. Since their bodies were light, almost shadowy, as had been those of Amelius and other early souls, they could come and go in the instant required for thought projection.

Excitedly recalling the strange visitations described by the Biblical Ezekiel, I asked for more information about these spacemen, and the Guides wrote, "By manipulating atoms they could appear and disappear at will, moving giant boulders in the same way by dismantling the atomic structure of stones and reassembling them on the site of their choosing. It was a demonstration to earthlings of what they could again achieve if they too divorced themselves from the physical magnet of earth and became as thought forms, lighter than air. Intricate drawings of these atomic disassemblers were left behind in various places, drawn not by the humans who saw them but by these so-called gods from outer space, in the hope that future generations, understanding the intricacy of the work, could also reproduce the patterns of energy that would enable them to dissolve and reassemble the atomic structures of rocks and other objects. This is the way the great pyramids of Giza and elsewhere were assembled. It is the way Jesus left the tomb without trace of his body."

I wanted to know if the space travelers were real to the touch, and the Guides continued: "Yes, in exactly the same way that your astronauts are real to the touch on the moon, were there any inhabitants on that burned-out body to touch them. Yes, they ate and talked and sang and performed as men do everywhere, but the secret of their success was that they could dissolve and reassemble atomic structures, and in outer space could project themselves as thought patterns until they entered the heavier density of the earth pull, at which time machinery and protective wrappings were needed to cope with the magnetic pull. In this manner we nowadays continue to see UFOs which mysteriously appear and disappear, for they too respond to the magnetism of the earth and need heavier-than-air machines to transport themselves here, but in the outer stratosphere can travel almost instantaneously."

Certainly if the Guides are correct, these visitations could explain the many drawings carved on rocks and within ancient caves depicting astronaut-like beings conversing with earth men and women. In such widely separated areas as the Sahara, Peru (which the Guides say was a part of Lemuria), Africa, Europe, and America are cave drawings with figures of animals and men, beside whom stand other figures sporting what appear to be antennae on their heads, wearing bulky space suits and holding mechanical boxes. Some even wear helmets resembling those of our own astronauts. Are they actually self-portraits drawn by ancient spacemen? Did Ezekiel truly witness the landing of spaceships? We know that the Bible is replete with accounts of visitations from angels who suddenly appeared to bring wise counsel to Old Testament characters. Could some have been spacemen from more highly developed planets who were taking an interest in earth's development?

The Guides say that "the earliest souls brought with them the science of mathematics, which is a divine law of harmony and balance," and assuredly they understood the computations of astronomy, because near Biblical Nineveh is an ancient example with fifteen digits that would defy our modern computers. They also had "perfect knowledge of the law of harmony in music," although the tones reproduced by reeds or larnyx were less lyrical than those heard in the spirit state.

The fascinating experiment on tiny Planet Earth continued to attract souls into physical bodies, and as the population flourished on Mu, adventurous ones cast forth in ships to explore other parts of the globe. Some went to what were then slim stretches of land in today's North and South America, and since there was an open strait between the two segments, they sailed freely to Atlantis through what is now the isthmus and the Caribbean.

Atlantis was then a semitropical paradise peopled by the Red race, and also by animal-like humans with grotesque bodies who descended from the perpetrators of Original Sin. Unlike the Lemurians who had schooled and uplifted their monstrous ones, however, the Atlanteans treated theirs as beasts of burden who performed only the most menial tasks. The Guides seemed anxious to tell more about life on Atlantis, but before leaving the subject of Mu, I had a few more questions. What, for instance, was civilization like in those faraway times? With alacrity they responded:

"Civilization reached an extraordinary peak in those days of spiritual awareness. Education was at such fantastic levels that each adult had the equivalent of a Ph.D. degree today, and many far exceeded it in their perception and ideals. The government of Mu was smooth and unhurried. Those who shared in its day-to-day operation had little to do, for there was no welfare, no crime, no hatred. If one person had a temporary grievance against another, an arbitrator talked with each of them separately and then together, so that they could understand both points of view. No one was confined to prisons, and none would have regarded it as punishment anyway, since by use of thought power he could have withdrawn from it. Even when bodies became denser so that one could not physically escape, his mind would have re-created the pleasures of the out-of-doors, and only the shell or body would have remained incarcerated while the soul wandered freely wherever it wished. Thus punishment for a misdemeanor consisted of helping that person to understand the nature of his offense, so that it would not be repeated. The anguish of being made an example for special care was sufficient to deter that soul from another such trepass."

I asked when the law of karma, the Biblical "eye for an eye, tooth for a tooth" went into effect, and the Guides said there had always been such a law, even before souls entered physical body. "Divine law will not be thwarted," they wrote, "and when one violates that law, he must repay, or be cut off from the creative force we term God. This knowledge entered with Amelius and his associates, and so freshly was it engraved on their souls that to violate the law was to fall from grace. As we have told you, some yielded to temptation by embracing animals or other nonhuman species, and in doing so incurred evil karma which followed them out of the body and into the next one, after God shortened the life-span. Returning as Adams and Eves and other early beings, they sought to erase their karmic indebtedness by gentle rule over the animal kingdom, but Lucifer welcomed this opportunity to take command of those who erred against God's will. This fallen angel offered an endless supply of pleasures, taunting the souls with their labors when they could loll in the grass and partake of the fruits of others. Thus he came into his own realm, and in the countless millenia since, he has never lacked for subjects in his kingdom. The strife fomented by this fallen angel has upset the workings of God's plan over and over again, until it sometimes would seem that he is more powerful than the Creator; yet this is untrue, for when a soul turns from evil ways and looks again to the Father, miracles await. God is all powerful, and will pursue an errant one time out of mind, capturing his faith again, if not in one lifetime, then in the next, for until man is rid of the devil's entrapment he will not again see God.

"Thus we have reincarnation, the sad story of man returning again and again to physical body, resolved to wash out the evil from his record. Some have advanced sufficiently to complete the wheel of rebirth, and these perfected ones need never return to physical body."

One day the Guides drew a fascinating analogy between souls and planets. They said God fashioned planets and suns to light the dark void, and as they spun into orbit, developing each in its own manner, some were able to support life and others were not. We are the same, they said, for as we entered the earth we developed in own manner, "some barren, some fertile, some full of marvelous ideas, and others merely plodders putting one foot before another.

"People are planets," they declared, "and some are starred with brilliance while others spin endlessly in space, without thought or creative design. God furnished each planet according to its potential, some with trees and verdant plains, others with gases, minerals, crystalline powder, water, or sand. To each planet was left the development of its plant life or other atomic structure. Planets are simply larger replicas of atoms, and we are like planets each with its own field of endeavor. Thus humans, like planets, were permitted to develop in their own way, and some have realized their true potential while others occupy a wasteland within."

The Guides say that on Mu there was only one form of religion—adoration of the Creator—and as seafaring Lemurians explored the world, they took with them the knowledge handed down from the beginning, as preserved by the high priests. Some of their sailing vessels reached Atlantis, where they found kindred souls whose civilization had also become highly developed in the tens of thousands of years since the advent of homo sapiens. But the Atlanteans were much more inventive than the visiting Lemurians, who were astounded by the luxurious life-style and the machines that operated labor-saving devices.

We will hear a great deal more about Atlantean

inventions in subsequent chapters, but meanwhile I was prompted to ask what kind of sports were popular in Lemura and Atlantis. The Guides replied that the favorites on Mu were the decathlon type, principally running and spear-throwing. "Atlanteans," they said, "favored more warlike games, with sides being chosen and the players hurling themselves at each other in combat. Sometimes a football field today looks like an Atlantean sport when a tackle has been made, and many are lying in a heap on the ground. There were then no ball games, because the ball like the wheel was developed much later, although the ancient ball courts in Mexico and elsewhere in the Americas stemmed from a type of rock-throwing in some matches on Atlantis."

4

Descent from the Angels

Civilization on Mother Earth has never again equaled the towering heights achieved in those golden years on Lemuria and Atlantis. Most of the people were high-minded, and due to their industrious bent, the land was covered with luxuriant vegetation. But not all was idyllic. Thanks to the succulence created through man's endeavors, some species were reproducing even more rapidly than the human race. Giant birds and mammals attacked the crops, enormous lizards crawled out of the sea to stalk the land, and the dinosaurs with their gigantic bodies and tiny brains struck with such ferocity that people began banding together in tightly guarded communities. On Mu the danger was so great that Lemurians had to dig shelters beneath the earth, or enlarge caves in the hillsides to escape the predatory beasts.

The Guides give a graphic description of this lamentable era, writing, "In the land of Lemuria were giant dinosaurs who roamed the plains and struck down forests in their wake, destroying crops and uprooting orchards that had been tenderly nurtured for food and shade. They trampled on all within range—one toe could crush a small child— and fought mighty battles among themselves over such tasty morsels as man and smaller beasts."

For some reason I had been under the impression that dinosaurs were herbivorous. Always eager to catch my mysterious informants in a misstatement of fact, I therefore checked the *Encyclopædia Britannica* and read that indeed many kinds of dinosaurs were flesh-eating. Unperturbed by my impolite doubts, the Guides continued: "Their great tails lashed through brush and stream, bent only on seeking food and shelter from mighty storms that occasionally swept the burgeoning earth."

Since Edgar Cayce had also spoken of the contest between early man and giant animals, I asked for an illustration of conditions at that time, and the Guides wrote, "Let us consider the life of one family on Lemuria. They lived in a cave sheltered from wild animals, and all that the women were able to see were shadows cast by those who passed the open entrance. Thus it was a shadow world, and although some retained memories of their life in spirit, others having heard such stories thought that the shadows were spirits of other-world entities and conversed freely with them, not realizing that the physical body casting the shadow stood between them and the daylight at their back. Women and children seldom ventured forth from the entrance due to the fear of animals too big for today's comprehension. The men emerged only to seek game, for this was principally a meat-eating time after the herbs growing in the immediate vicinity of the caves and mounds had been uprooted.

"These were the days of cave dwellers, and many were the art forms expressed on cavern walls during the tedious days when there was little to occupy the men and women. Walls were blackened by the fires from cookery. Thus many of these artistic creations drawn near the surface were lost, although some carved more deeply made a lasting imprint. A family called Endymius dwelt with others in a somewhat larger cave than most, which offered more social contact. Children born there seldom saw the light of day and ended their life-span within the confines of the cave, although occasionally when hunters reported no sight of huge beasts, they did venture forth, blinking painfully in the brilliant sunshine and staring for miles across the open plains.

"These families intermarried in brief ceremonies performed by the priestly caste composed of those who could recall spirit life. One of these holy men or women would ask the young couple to join hands while all chanted in unison the blessing of the clan. All shared in the cooking after men had captured a hare, otter, small game, or occasional buffalo. They ate, they slept, they propagated, they talked, and this was the molelike existence of these hapless Lemurians.

"Thus man knew descent from the angels, and until some of the hardy ones began feeble efforts to eradicate the fearsome beasts, there seemed little hope for mankind."

At a later date the Guides told of another Lemurian family which numbered twenty, including grandchildren. They lived beneath a mound in an apartment hollowed out of the ground, with a crawl-through opening to prevent large beasts from entering. They slept on reed mats woven from the tall grasses growing nearby, and the family ate nuts and berries, with the addition of meat that the men could occasionally spear nearby.

"This would be some sixty thousand years ago," the Guides continued. "The family lived in semi-darkness except for the light from the opening and from tapers made of the fat of animal carcasses, which smoked so badly that they were used mainly in emergency. One day while the men were out hunting, a huge dinosaur sniffed its way to the concealed entrance, and with its brutish head tried to force a wider opening. All within were terrified, but with a rare burst of courage the children grabbed clubs and began beating its head while smoke belched from its mouth. The fathers, hearing the vibration of its terrible roar, rushed to the scene and with their spears stabbed the creature hundreds of times before it lay dying. Dozens of men from neighboring caves and mounds were then required to drag the carcass far enough away so that its rotting would not contaminate the area, or attract other beasts. Thus these families lived out their days, bearing children, raising and feeding them under such terrible stress that their earthly lives were foreshortened. Always they yearned for the beauty of the outside world, even as an ailing oldster now yearns for passage to what you call heaven."

Virtually the only untrammeled souls on Mu in those dreadful times were fishermen, since the seacoasts were too sparse of vegetation to attract the mammoths and dinosaurs. Yet the continent was so heavily populated that most could not take advantage of that freedom. "Thus it was a momentous day when the first flying ship landed on the lagoon of Chalda in Lemuria," the Guides declare, "bringing hope to these unfortunate descendants of highly cultured beings who had now descended nearly to the level of beasts, through their aimless lives in semidarkness. The memory of the original language brought from the spirit realm of pure thought made it possible for the Lemurians to understand the Atlantean visitors, although many words were different because of long usage in separated continents, and when they comprehended that the Atlanteans wished their cooperation in convening a worldwide congress to talk of ways to rid the earth of its gargantuan creatures, they were overjoyed."

The Guides then skipped to the conferences, but

I later clamored for more details about the dramatic first visit, and they wrote, "When the first airborne Atlanteans stepped foot on Mu, it was as if a fire fanned out across the world, dispelling the lethargy of the ages. They greeted the Lemurians like ones who had reclaimed their brothers, and some of the sailors who had visited Atlantis by ship were particularly excited because they had been aware of the project to build planes, but had not dared hope to see it put into operation. The spacecraft was able to set down on the flat wide beach, and since animals of enormous size did not inhabit that sandy area there was no immediate danger. Word of the landing was spread by means of a kind of grapevine developed long before, which responded to the vibrations of instruments hewn from wood. These were somewhat akin to African tribal drums, and when one heard the message, it was passed along by similar drums to others for hundreds of miles. Thus the Lemurians sped to the area to greet the visitors, and what a gladsome time it was! Atlanteans recounted stories of the wonders to be found in their land, and Lemurians wept at the contrast between the luxury of Atlantis and the poverty of Mu, where so many lived in semidarkness. It was like describing the wonders of New York or London to an African Pygmy who has never ventured beyond his mud village. Atlanteans were appalled by the dark and dingy mounds to which they were taken for safety during their stay, and Lemurian elders gladly agreed to return with them to Atlantis where others would be gathering from lands beyond the seas. Since Atlantis was now able to send ships and balloons with increasing facility, some young people were taken along to learn engineering and chemical skills.

"Drofus was the name of the pilot commanding the plane, and with him were two scientists who understood the maneuvers by which the craft would attach itself to a particular facet of the Crystal and direct the passage of other ships through that beam or ray from the Great Crystal, without dropping speed or losing contact. An intricate process indeed, and one which is not understood today, but will one day be used again to propel planes and ships. In taking off from Lemuria or another area removed from Atlantis, delicate preparations were necessary, including the synchronizing of smaller crystals within the craft until finely tuned into the particular ray of the Great Crystal that would beckon it home. Since the principle was buried with lost Atlantis, we are not aware of how it was performed, except to marvel at its proficiency."

The Guides say that at one of the international gatherings "wise heads hit upon the idea" of ferreting out the young of the beasts and destroying them while still in the infant stage. Creative Atlanteans then devised a toxic gas that could be "blown into the breeding grounds" when the wind was right, and it proved effective on the young, although it was insufficiently powerful to eradicate grown animals. The Guides also described a curious instrument "somewhat like a dowsing rod in more sophisticated form" which helped men "at tremendous peril" locate the breeding grounds of mastodons and dinosaurs, and thereafter brave people sought out their lairs in many parts of the world.

Atlanteans of this era were apparently a kindly people, because after learning of the wretched living conditions forced on Lemurians by the giant animals, they urged some to migrate to their own country, and they taught others how to construct sturdier boats for the much longer passage westward to what is now Asia. But the Atlanteans shared with no other race the secrets of the giant Crystal, about which the sleeping Edgar Cayce spoke at length, that propelled their aircraft and submarines.

"Hundreds of years were devoted to the war against the dinosaurs and other mammoth creatures," the Guides wrote, "and many were the international conclaves held to discuss faster ways of freeing the land, before the cataclysm came that solved the problem. Little time was required to assemble elders from various countries, because Atlanteans came for them in their flying craft or balloons."

This latter statement fascinated me. Could it perhaps explain those geometrically patterned roads running parallel and intersecting others, which are plainly visible from the air above the plain of Nazca in Peru's Palpa Valley? Erich von Däniken speculates in *Chariots of the Gods* that they were for the use of outer-space beings, but when I eagerly asked the Guides about them, they wrote:

"As to those landing fields, there were many equally as great in various sections of Lemuria and Atlantis, and Peru was then a part of Mu. Some Atlantean flying machines needed less than a city lot for landing, since they were lightweight contraptions holding no more than two or four people that took off with attached balloon and could be regulated by an instrument controlling the drift of the wind. These were somewhat similar to today's helicopters, except for the balloon attachment, and were used for short hops. But the more powerful aircraft controlled by laser-like beams from the Crystal needed long runways, as do your jets today. Thus airports were built in various parts of the world to accommodate the craft flying in to gather elders for convocations, or to bring supplies of manufactured goods, for Atlantis by then was the undisputed world leader in the field of manufacturing and invention. Lemuria in her latter days was regarded as a mother, wise and gentle, who tried to school the colonies in manners and mores, but her wisdom seemed more philosophical than practical to her frisky offspring, who delighted in the more modern ways of Atlantis. Does that remind you of American youngsters today?"

Returning to the subject matter that I had interrupted with my query, they declared, "Man was making some headway in diminishing the herds of giant beasts even before the cataclysm that raised mountains throughout the world and destroyed

Lemuria. When one species endangers all others, his time on earth is limited. Let that be a warning to man, who is polluting the land, the sea, and the air to the detriment of all other species."

Intrigued by their cautionary note, I asked why God permitted the destruction of creatures he himself had created, and the Guides replied, "We are always undergoing experimentation. Many early species which became a scourge to others have since disappeared from Planet Earth. Even so, man will one day disappear in physical form if he continues to pollute the earth. Live and let live is the universal law, and when one species assumes a destructive role, his time on earth is short-lived, for unless we are helping others there is no place in God's plan for that species or individual. Think on this."

Another time, puzzling about the monstrous dinosaurs whose bones continue to be unearthed in some areas of the world, I asked how God happened to make such a mistake of creation.

"God does not make mistakes," my Guides retorted, "but like any intelligent being made in his image he experiments, and gives each idea a thorough testing before withdrawing it. Men at first were more than ten feet tall, or shorter than three feet, but the stature has since been modulated to an average of five or so feet. You will note that man is again growing taller than in recent millenia, so perhaps there is purpose for that in today's environment. But man, like the dinosaurs, will be withdrawn if he becomes a menace, rather than merely a pest as of now. Experimentation in creation is still continuing, for nothing is static."

I stupidly asked what became of the souls of dinosaurs after they ceased to exist in the physical realm, and the Guides responded: "The records at our disposal do not show that, because they had no individual souls. It is man who writes the akashic records on the skein of time."

As the great herds of the beasts began gradually to diminish, humans once again were able to walk in the sun and the wind, but many on Mu were compelled to continue living in underground mounds because of overcrowded surface conditions. So great was the population explosion in the many thousands of years after life became more livable on Mu that the colonization of less populated continents continued in earnest. "Lemurians were quick to spread the worship of the one true God, for they had not strayed from that supreme knowledge, and those saintly ones who led the expeditions and migrations to other areas of the world kept pure the faith and the knowledge of creation. They carefully trained the younger ones, who passed along the knowledge to each succeeding generation, and for many millenia this knowledge flourished until gradually it became adulterated by the false religions of primitive tribes. Those dwelling in forests worshiped spirits who gave them protection from animals, and those who husbanded crops worshiped sun and rain spirits, so that they began to replace in the minds of those primitive peoples the almighty Creator, the one and only God who created the spirits as well as the earth, the sun, and the rain."

Where in the world, I wondered, did primitive tribes come from, if man simultaneously appeared on five continents? Apparently reading my thoughts the Guides wrote, "Almost from the beginning there were souls in the earth less advanced than others, having wasted their opportunities even while spirit entities. They too found their way into human vehicles, some to families who had set off into isolated areas. These souls, long separated from social contact with those more closely linked, retrogressed rapidly, as they had little stimulus for mental growth, and when they were encountered by migrating Lemurians, they seemed backward in their customs and ideology. This was many millenia after the advent of man in human form."

I asked if the Guides could tell me anything more about childrearing in Lemuria, and they replied that in the Golden Age before animals became so prolific, children were trained by those who recalled spirit life and were in communication with spirits as freely as we speak with a neighbor. The youngsters were taught the reasons for their venture into physical body and the good that would be achieved through fulfillment of divine laws. Each knew his place in the scheme of things, and for that reason there was no violence and no revolt. Parents understood that these little ones were souls as old as themselves, who had chosen them as parents to learn the lessons of the flesh, and they were therefore regarded as peers. Each was introduced to the laws of harmony, mathematics, music, reading and writing; and the Lemurians had literature of high quality.

The insular living brought on by the cave-dwelling and mound-building days sadly reduced the level of intelligence, but contact with Atlanteans again raised the quality of thought, opening a window on the world, and those who had kept alive the flame of spirituality and philosophy found new reaches for the mind. The Lemurians were never an inventive people, but the superlative development of a philosophy for living and their dedication to divine laws made them the world's leaders in goodness and thought.

"These children of Mu were perhaps the most perfect beings of all the world's peoples," the Guides concluded, "since they scarcely knew the meaning of sin against parents, teachers, or companions."

The discussion of children prompted me to request more information about those stalwart Lemurian women who, according to the Guides, bore "dozens of children" during their long lives. "Child-bearing was painless and no assistance was needed," they wrote, "as women considered it a normal occurrence and had no morbid hang-ups about it. Does a wild animal require assistance to whelp? Do mammals need to be taught to nurse their young? Have you heard of birds weeping when eggs are laid? So it was with homo sapiens on Mu."

My mysterious Guides sounded so all-knowing that I asked if they had ever lived on Lemuria, and they obligingly replied, "Yes, some of us were among those on Mu in the latter days after the beasts had begun to disappear, and we recall specific occasions when we saw the landing of lighter-than-air craft from Atlantis, and the setting forth of ships from Mu."

Then, to my immense relief, they added, "We find that you, Ruth, were not among those on Lemuria, but that the first physical life for you was in Atlantis. Many of those living today were on Atlantis rather than Mu, for souls have a tendency to reincarnate in cycles with companions they have known before in earth life, and when one cycle is completed, another begins for a different group. There is naturally some overlapping of periods, depending on a person's life-span, and there are numerous different cycles from Atlantis, Lemuria, ancient Mongolia, Persia, et cetera."

Perhaps this explains why I have encountered such unusual difficulty in writing these early chapters. Very little of it seems to click with me, and like any good newspaper reporter I can write a more vivid account when I have actually witnessed the action.

5

Airships of Antiquity

"Now let us go to Atlantis."

With those words the Guides began a morning session, and I felt instant relief. Perhaps at last I could begin to relate to the strange material they were divulging.

"It was a magical continent," they continued, "more ideal than any before or since, with virgin forests, undulating plains, rills, brooks, and a mighty river separating Poseidia from the remainder of the landmass. Truly a land of milk and honey! Amelius and his lighter-than-air companions were familiar with this verdant paradise, visiting it frequently, but why they chose Lemuria over Atlantis we are unable to say, since that was

before akashic records were imprinted on the skein
of time. The real history of Atlantis began when
the sexes were divided, and the so-called Adams
had their Eves."

The Guides have a maddening way of hopping
blithely from one era to another, and I became
hopelessly confused when they abruptly plunged
into the governmental structure of Atlantis, writing
that it was ruled by a king named Atlas and his
many descendants. Who, I demanded to know,
was Atlas? And when did he arrive on Atlantis?

I could sense their astonishment at my naïveté
as they replied, "Atlas was the name for Adam in
Atlantis, and his wife was Heputh. Poseidon was
their name for Amelius or one of his counterparts
in the earliest time; we are unsure of which, for
no akashic records show that."

Somewhat mollified, I permitted them to proceed
and they wrote, "Atlantis stretched from the east
rim of the Americas, including coastal parts of
Georgia, the Carolinas, Virginia, the West Indies,
and Brazil, across what is now ocean nearly to
the west coast of Africa. The first rulers were
highly developed souls who still recalled spirit existence and were therefore able to utilize that
knowledge of thought communication. On Atlantis
were powerful forces which originated with Atlas
and ran through currents of energy to all with
whom he came in contact, so that the enlightened
ones were able to sense his thoughts without the
necessity of writing or reading. It was the language
of symbology, and as he projected these pictures

by means of energy rays from his mind, the entire community worked as one."

I asked if this represented a form of hypnosis and they replied in the negative, saying, "It was simply the energy of thought, as available today as it was then, but sadly disused. As this powerful force spread from Atlas through his family, it became a living energy, and from it emerged mighty inventions that have not been equaled since the destruction of that continent, for Atlas would project the thought pattern, and others through like understanding of the thought waves could help bring it into physical being. Thus, as the peoples of Atlantis continued to use this force throughout thousands of years, the inventive core became foremost, and those who later developed aircraft, submarines, boats, and electrical rays somewhat akin to today's laser beams produced the most technically advanced civilization ever known to man."

Skipping backward to the early beginnings of homo sapiens on Atlantis the Guides continued: "Atlas begat numerous sons and daughters who were of such exalted temperament that each gave enlightened rule to his or her portion of the continent and adjoining land areas. Parts of the British Isles were then a governmental segment of Atlantis, before the series of cataclysms that inundated land bridges leading to it, to Portugal and West Africa. These enlightened princes had their own domains, and Atlas was a court of last resort in the event of disputes. In those days man lived such aeons of time that the question of succession had not yet arisen, and before long there were hundreds of living descendants of Atlas. His wife Heputh was, of course, the other half of his soul and she effortlessly gave birth to two dozen children, each of whom had many offspring, so that there was no dearth of leadership in that happy isle."

This account, I later discovered to my surprise, differs only slightly from that of Plato, the illustrious Greek scholar who bequeathed to the Western world our oldest history of Atlantis. Plato obtained his knowledge of the fabled lost continent from Solon, the great Athenian lawgiver of 600 B.C., who during ten years spent in Egypt learned the story of Atlantis from wise men and priests of Sais, the ancient capital of Lower Egypt. According to Plato's account, a god Poseidon begat five sets of male twins by a "mortal woman." The eldest, Atlas, became king and himself sired a large family which continued to rule over the empire for many centuries. The Guides emphasized, however, that Atlas and his descendants were a "pure strain never profaned by cohabitation with animal-like Things or Manators" who had existed on Atlantis long before the advent of the Atlas dynasty. These grotesque beings were treated by Atlanteans like beasts of burden, yoked to plows, used to draw water from wells, and in later times harnessed to machinery.

The Guides claim that although a division existed between the two classes of beings, none at first felt abused because each was serving as best he could. "But during the ensuing tens of thousands of years strife arose between the two class systems and also among homo sapiens, who had lost the sense of kinship and oneness. Atlas and his immediate descendants by then were long gone, and the land was plentifully peopled, although the giant birds and beasts that had developed apace were threatening to exterminate mankind."

As a newspaper reporter accustomed to dealing with facts, I was having difficulty in accepting the assertions of Edgar Cayce and the Guides that men began as shadowy beings who gradually became more solid while inhabiting the earth. From whence came the physical substance? The Guides offered this explanation: "Man began as thought form, but when he entered animals and produced the Things, he became entrapped in the earth. When God created man and woman as separate parts of the whole soul, he used materials of the earth to fashion their earthly bodies, as he had done with the animals and all other living things, for the basic ingredients of earthlings are the same —gases, air, water, minerals, vitamins, and soil. These human beings were the ultimate creation, but made of the same materials as those thought-into-being by the Supreme Diety for everything on this planet. Do not visualize the creation as two large hands reaching down from heaven and gathering up clay, with which were mixed water and mineral and vegetable. Rather, it was the *idea* of God to use materials suitable to this particular planet, to mold into being through his almighty thought the ingredients to fashion a perfect being."

Having disposed of that subject at least to their own satisfaction, the Guides declared that Atlantis for many millenia was ruled by a succession of wise kings and princes who worked together for the common good. "Yet like the American South in the golden days of plantations there were ugly seeds within, for the Atlanteans mistreated the Things [as they called their half-human, half-animal work force] just as some Dixie planters did the Blacks who had been captured in Africa and enslaved—a terrible thing to do to another. These Encumbered Souls mostly cohabited with each other, so the strain was not improving, and they dwelt mainly in hovels while the Atlantean Red race lived in luxury, with every imaginable kind of labor-saving device operated by crystals which harnessed the sun's energy. They were a creative society, fond of experimentation with all sorts of gases, minerals, and plants, and they used the Things for toting, pushing, hauling, and even managing some projects under the supervision of the Atlanteans."

The Guides report that Beings from outer space were particularly attracted to Atlantis because of the inventive bent of its race, and spent much time there communing with them. "This is not as ridiculous as it may sound to earth people today," the Guides insisted, "because there were no time or space barriers. Thought patterns easily came into physical being before the molten core of the earth became so magnetized that souls were trapped by its gravity. These space visitors proved helpful in designing the mighty Crystal which in the beginning was a tremendous force for good, launching ships that flew or swam or were propelled across the surface of the ocean at fantastic speeds, before it was used destructively."

The mighty Crystal! That force for good and evil which Edgar Cayce said still lies beneath the Atlantic Ocean in the Bermuda Triangle, where so many planes and ships have mysteriously disappeared in recent decades. I could scarcely wait to ask the Guides more about it, and at the next morning's session they obligingly wrote:

"Visiting space people told Atlanteans how to prepare the giant Crystals after they had already begun to harness energy with smaller crystals that operated labor-saving devices. From a hillside on Atlantis they found a vein of quartz sufficient in size to reflect all rays of the sun and moon, for the moon had its part to play in this tremendous experiment. By cutting away the earth from all sides, they then etched facets so delicate as to reflect every ray, and since there was nothing in the atmosphere in those pristine days to deflect the sun's rays, they had constant use of the Crystal except during occasional rains. By producing more energy than essential to each day's usage, they found a way to store the energy in copper vats so that no plane or ship depended on one day's energy supply to propel it on proper course."

I am so abysmally ignorant of anything having

to do with mechanics or chemistry that I was unaware of the relationship between quartz and crystal until I consulted a dictionary. There I read that "quartz, or silicon dioxide occurring in crystals, is one of the commonest minerals. It is piezoelectric and is cut into wafers used to control the frequencies of radio transmitters." I further learned that piezoelectric means electricity produced by pressure "as in a crystal subjected to compression along a certain axis."

After digesting this information, I asked the Guides to continue their discussion of the Crystal, and they wrote, "These space visitors arrived in airships of remarkable design thought-into-being by highly advanced minds in the spirit plane, for until they reached the earth's atmosphere they had no need of machinery, and earth time is nonexistent beyond our atmosphere. Then they would produce the electrical components out of earth products that had been turned into gaseous elements. It sounds farfetched, but the records are here to prove it.

"With these machines as a prototype, the Atlanteans quickly put together similar craft composed of solids capable of being propelled by energy from the Crystal in all directions, depending on the facets left uncovered for a particular journey. Some who worked on the inventions were souls who had previously been in the earth plane as shadow-like forms and well understood the power of the mind. Others followed their patterns and soon demonstrated that the will is more powerful than the idea, for it is easier to invent something if you know in advance that it will work. Seeing machines brought to earth by outer-space beings proved the workability, and all doubt was therefore removed. It is so even today. When one nation discovers atomic power and demonstrates its practical application, it is less difficult for another nation to produce it, knowing that it is a workable project."

According to the Guides, the fact that huge beasts and birds overrunning the earth compelled Atlanteans to live together in walled cities or compounds gave impetus to their inventive genius, because they spent much time talking to each other.

"Requirement is ever the mother of invention," they wrote, "and those Atlanteans who had descended from original lighter-than-air souls and retained their faculty for conversing with the spirit realm through a form of meditation took the lead in developing wonders the world had never seen. Some felt that to fly as a bird should be easy, since some of those Things about them had wings and feathers, so they tried to devise a machine that would duplicate the feat of the giant fowl who had been ancestors of these half-bird beings. Then a happening occurred that changed the life of the early world. Spacemen landed on Atlantis in such numbers as to prove that man would be able to fly with a proper understanding of aerodynamics. They came in planes of varying pattern, but most had discs and whirling engines to defy the law of gravity both in take-off and landing."

I asked why they favored Atlantis rather than Lemuria or more isolated areas, and the Guides wrote, "Because like always attracts like, and these spacemen who recognized the inquiring minds and inventive genius of the Atlanteans felt more welcome there. Today they are appearing again in parts of the world where man's inventive powers have proven an attraction. Seldom is a UFO seen in backward rural countries, but primarily near cities in such advanced inventive nations as America, Israel, and Germany."

Dr. Philip Cressy, Jr., a scientist at Goddard Space Center who firmly believes that there are other civilizations than ours in the universe, says, "I can't overlook the possibility that we may have had visitors from outer space. There is no evidence to tell me it cannot or has not happened." A recent Gallup Poll indicates that half the U.S. population believes the same, and Jesse Lawrence, an investigator for the National Investigations Committee for Aerial Phenomena, said he is convinced that this planet has been visited by aircraft from outer space. "There's no doubt about UFOs," Lawrence declares, "and I think we also had visitors from outer space aeons ago."

The Guides claim that while visiting spacemen exchanged ideas with Atlanteans on the best ways to defeat the earth's pull of gravity, "one of them hit upon the idea of a crystal so finely chiseled as to absorb the sun's rays for a new form of energy. There was an ample supply of quartz, and for many years the Atlanteans experimented with various sizes and types until they began to capture nature's secret of collective energy, and as lesser crystals began propelling small objects, they commenced work on a crystal so large and so pure that it would direct all objects in whatsoever direction propelled. Many years were required to prepare this enormous crystal, while also building the proper reflector in which to house it. With this accomplished they began the laborious task of erecting a shelter with a domed, movable top so that the energy could be directed where desired. Spacemen were enchanted with the progress and gave many helpful suggestions, particularly in plans for various types of craft to be propelled by the harnessed energy. Some craft flew, some swam beneath the waters, and others hovered almost motionless high above objects being studied from the air. In this way they mapped vast areas of the world, and some of these maps came to light many generations ago, showing the earth before the last polar shift when the Antarctic was free of ice."

Fantastic, if true! This then would explain those amazing maps found in Turkey early in the 1700s. The property of Turkish Admiral Piri Reis, they were copies of extremely ancient maps clearly delineating mountain ranges on Antarctica in an ice-free age, mountains that modern cartographers could not map until 1952 with the aid of sophisticated echo-sounding devices. Since Reis' maps accurately portray the earth contours when transferred to a modern globe, and are amazingly similar to aerial photographs taken from today's satellites, Professor Charles H. Hapgood and mathematician Richard W. Strachan conclude that the Reis maps must have been aerial photographs made from great heights above the earth's surface. Even the distortion of continents lying farther from the center of the picture is duplicated in the shots taken by our U.S. astronauts.

During a discussion of the Reis maps in a radio broadcast by the Georgetown University Forum on August 26, 1956, it was stated that such a mapping feat would seem impossible of accomplishment without the aid of aerial surveys. The participants were Reverend Daniel Linehan, S.S., director of Western Observatory of Boston College, a seismologist who participated in U.S. Navy explorations of Antarctica; Mr. I. I. Walters, a cartographer who was formerly with the U.S. Hydrographic office, and Mr. A. H. Mallery, an authority on ancient maps who "discovered" the Reis maps in the Library of Congress and solved their projection. *Edgar Cayce on Atlantis,* a book by Edgar Evans Cayce, reports in some detail on the accuracy of these ancient maps.

Certainly no one was flying in the early eighteenth century, when the Reis maps came to light, but Edgar Cayce and the Guides agree that the Atlanteans were high fliers!

6

Evidence of Atlantis

If one approaches the subject with open mind, there seems to be more proof than disproof for the existence of a once-great landmass in the Atlantic Ocean. Nearly twenty-four hundred years ago Plato ascribed its location "to the west of the straits which you call the Pillars of Hercules," our present-day Straits of Gibraltar. He said it was "larger than Libya and Asia put together, and from it could be reached other islands, and from the islands you might pass through to the opposite continent [i.e., America] which surrounded the true ocean; for this sea [i.e., the Mediterranean] which is within the columns of Hercules is only a harbour, having a narrow entrance, but that other is a real sea, and the surrounded land may be most truly called a continent." Plato added that it "was called Atlantis and was the heart of a great and wonderful empire, which had rule over the whole island and several others, as well as over parts of the continent."

After describing the life-style of the Atlanteans as told to Solon, Plato said that "when afterward sunk by an earthquake" Atlantis "became an impassable barrier of mud to voyagers sailing from hence to the ocean." Historians record that for thousands of years the Ancients considered the Atlantic Ocean a shallow, muddy, dark sea. Edgar Cayce while in trance reported that Atlantis broke apart and eventually disappeared during three widely separated cataclysms, the last in approximately 10,000 B.C. Plato was obviously referring to the final destruction, whose date he similarly estimated.

Is it really so strange that a body of land should disappear beneath the sea and be virtually forgotten in twelve thousand years? Geologists testify that our present continents and islands have undergone countless alterations, rising and sinking over aeons of time. The shores of Norway, Sweden, and Denmark have risen several hundred feet during recent millenia. Sicily, now three thousand feet above sea level, once was ocean floor. Coal deposits in Pennsylvania prove that the area has been above or below water level at least twenty-three different times. The most devastating earthquake of modern times occurred two hundred years ago in Lisbon, Portugal (near the eastern coast of Lost Atlantis), killing sixty thousand people within six minutes. Many had fled for safety to a marble quay which suddenly sank six hundred feet below sea level, sucking down every person as well as numerous ships anchored nearby, and not one fragment ever emerged. Simultaneously the ground opened in a Moroccan village, swallowing all ten thousand inhabitants.

Violent volcanic eruptions have occurred in the Azores, which are thought to be remaining peaks of Atlantis, and also in the West Indies, which were western reaches of the Lost Continent. Many people living today can recall the eruption of Mont Pelée on Martinique in 1902, when the capital city's entire population of thirty thousand was wiped out in a matter of minutes, and of course the devastating earthquake in Guatemala within the past year.

Nearly forty years ago Edgar Cayce predicted that portions of Atlantis around Bimini would begin to reappear in 1968 or 1969, and within the past few years explorers and geologists have photographed formations just beneath the sea's surface there which resemble walls and buildings. In 1898 a French ship mending a broken cable north of the Azores found, at a depth of fifteen hundred fathoms, fragments of vitreous lava which could only have been formed in the atmosphere, since lava solidifying under water has a crystalline structure. Scientists who examined the lava fragments (now in the Paris Museum) concluded that since lava decomposes within fifteen thousand years, the area must have been above sea-level within that period.

Further evidence for a missing landmass between Europe and the Americas can be found in a report published in 1949 by Professor Maurice Ewing of Columbia University, an outstanding geologist who conducted explorations in the Atlantic Ocean, particularly in the area of the Mid-Atlantic Ridge. One of his many discoveries was prehistoric beach sand brought to the surface from depths up to three and one half miles, and as far distant from land as twelve hundred miles. Since sand is only formed on the surface, Professor Ewing concluded: "Either the land must have sunk two to three miles, or the sea once must have been two to three miles lower than now." It could not always have been sea bottom, nor would the theory of continental drift explain all that beach sand in the middle of the ocean.

Mountains, deep basins, and many layers of volcanic ash were found beneath the ocean by the expedition, and Professor Ewing reported: "In a depth of 3600 feet we found rocks that tell an interesting story about the past history of the Atlantic Ocean . . . granite and sedimentary rocks of types which originally must have been part of a continent. Most of the rocks that we dredged here were rounded and marked with deep scratches, or striations. But we also found some loosely consolidated mud stones . . . how they got out here is another riddle to be solved by further research." The Hudson River at the entrance to New York harbor was found to have a canyon running 120 miles along the continental shelf, plus another hundred miles into deep water. "If all this valley was originally carved out by the river on dry land, as seems probable," Ewing wrote, "it means either that the ocean floor of the Eastern seaboard of North America once must have stood about two miles above its present level and has since subsided, or else that the level of the sea was once about two miles lower than now." Certainly it is indicated that some prehistoric upheaval of catastrophic proportions inundated a vast segment of terra firma. For instance, geologists report that evidence of submerged caves reveals that the sea level of Bermuda at one time stood at least sixty to one hundred feet lower than at present.

The flora and fauna of our continents also give mute testimony to a once great landmass in the Atlantic Ocean. Perhaps the most impressive evidence is the banana which is seedless, and is not propagable by cuttings. Yet it is a plant that had to be cultivated a very long time to become seedless, and it grows profusely in the tropics of both Africa and the Americas. Banana roots cannot survive transporting through the Temperate Zone, so one can at least surmise that banana cultivation began on Atlantis, before spreading east and west to the adjoining African and American Tropics.

Recent scientific findings demonstrate that the horse originated in America, yet the animal was unknown to American Indians when Spanish conquerors brought it back to the New World in the sixteenth century. Did wild horses also cross through Atlantis to Europe and North Africa by way of land bridges in aeons past?

The North American continent in prehistoric times could have borne little resemblance to its present shape, because bones of whales have been found five or six hundred feet above sea level in such places as Michigan, New Hampshire, and Montreal. The remains of palms in northern Greenland prove that this area was once tropical, as does ancient coral unearthed in Alaska.

Many other such examples are enumerated in *Atlantis: The Antediluvian World* by Ignatius Donnelly, first published in 1882 and revised in 1949 by Egerton Sykes. Donnelly's book makes a compelling case for Atlantis by citing remarkable similarities between the culture of ancient Egypt and the Indian cultures of Central and South America as observed by Cortez and other Spanish conquerors: the nearly identical names of many cities, the towering pyramids, mutual legends of a mighty flood, a 365-day calendar, and the widespread use of the cross on religious edifices. These could all be a heritage from Atlantis that spread east and west from its shores.

Having personally explored numerous pyramids in Egypt and Mexico, I was so struck by their similarities, and by the use of crosses on temples in Mexico long before the Spanish conquistadores brought Christianity there, that I asked the Guides for an explanation, and they wrote, "From earliest times pyramids were built on Mu and Atlantis to represent man's reach for God, and in the days when there were no mountains, these were the highest spots for priests to worship the Creator and commune with his helpers. Always man thinks of God as above, in contrast to the earth beneath. The cross represented spiritual man in the earth with arms outstretched to either side, halfway between Planet Earth and the abode of the Creator."

I had another question about Mexico. Ever since reading William H. Prescott's *Conquest of Mexico* many years ago, I have been fascinated by the ease with which Hernando Cortez and his small, hardy band of Spanish conquistadores effected their landing, due to the fact that Emperor Moctezuma had long been expecting the "return" of bearded White men. According to Aztec legend, a tall, bearded White man called Quetzalcoatl once lived in Mexico, teaching the natives the art of government, agriculture, and metalworking. When the time came for him to depart, he sailed eastward through the Gulf of Mexico, promising to come back. The Mexicans, who had deified their benefactor, eagerly looked forward to his return, and consequently confused Cortez with Quetzalcoatl. The nearest landmass adjacent to the Gulf of Mexico would have been Atlantis, but the Guides as well as Edgar Cayce said that Atlantcans were of the Red race. How explain a White man sailing east?

The Guides gave this explanation: "Members of the White race first came to Atlantis at the time that conclaves were being held there to rid the world of dinosaurs and other monsters. When they saw the extraordinary beauty of that continent, they and delegates from other races spread the word, so that many migrated there and were made welcome. It was this seafaring White race, much later to be called Phoenicians, who eventually pushed onward to Mexico, not far distant from Atlantean shores, and they did indeed promise to return. But then came a Deluge that destroyed Atlantis, and they perished with it. Some of the Atlanteans, including Whites who had settled there, meanwhile had fled to Europe through the Pillars of Hercules, and there they established themselves, together with those Whites who had come from the Caucasus."

In the Golden Age of Atlantis, according to the Guides, people dwelt in lodgings similar to those of Roman times, using the natural stones, marbles, and clays as building materials. The perfect climate lent itself to open-air living, so that atriums, patios, and verandas were much in evidence. "The people were creative, fashioning new objects from mental pictures, and many Atlanteans had kept themselves sufficiently clear of evil that they could convey messages by thought projection faster than couriers could deliver them. This helps to explain why artistic creations were so similar in various parts of the world, for those early humans thought they were indelibly stamping the life and times of their people in rock, for all eternity. Many of their drawings depicted a type of Being that was relatively common at that time: the centaurs, unicorns, winged men, animal faces on human bodies, and human heads on animal bodies; yet many were striving to rid themselves of these deformities stemming from the time when cohabitation occurred between man and beast. As Atlanteans developed the power of the crystals, some of it was used to remove unwelcome appendages such as horns, tails, and claws, and progress was being made before the final cataclysm that destroyed Atlantis."

One morning before commencing the regular session, I asked why there seem to be so many more homosexuals today than in times past, and the Guides wrote, "Now as to the homosexuals who are coming out of the closet, as they phrase it: there were always those who felt more akinship with their own sex than the opposite one. This is a carry-over from previous lives in the opposite sexual body, for all are halves of complete souls. Today's frankness is airing the problem as never before since the days of Atlantis, when it was rampant, for in those earlier times many felt the pull of the other half of his soul, and through faithfulness to that other part of self which had not incarnated at that particular time, did not wish to cohabit with the opposite sex. These Atlanteans were accepted as a matter of course, some with admiration for their faithfulness, in fact; so do not be overly disturbed by the problem today. It is better, if one has that feeling of incompleteness, to resist the sexual impulse rather than cohabit with those of the same sex, but until mankind again reaches a state of perfection, there are many flaws to be overcome."

I asked the reason for reincarnation, and the Guides replied that in early days after the sexes were divided, "there were giants of overwhelming goodness who lived for such a long time that they came to be regarded as gods by others. But when God saw that some of them were succumbing to temptations and staining their once pure souls, he decreased the life-span in order to prevent havoc on the face of the earth. This gave these wayward souls a period of meditation in which to review their errors and determine to make amends, and when they were ready to try once more, they again were given opportunity to enter a physical body. Thus reincarnation was born, and it is as essential to man's development as the air that he breathes while in fleshly attire. When in physical body the souls yearn to rejoin their Creator. They are beset with homesickness for that state which is perfection, and although the way is steep and difficult to achieve, many, many souls have followed the path and have once again rejoined God as perfected souls who need not again return to physical body. Not all souls have incarnated, for free choice is given when opportunity avails. Some prefer from the spirit form to assist those who go into flesh, by helping them to reach their higher selves during meditation and dreams. Guardian angels? In a sense, yes, although they are souls who, lacking experience in earthly temptations, are solely seeking to remind those in bodily form to take the path of spiritual unfoldment."

The mention of guardian angels prompted me, at another time, to ask for an explanation of archangels. Are there such things, and if so, what are they? Perhaps this has no part in a discussion of Atlantis, but I was so fascinated by their reply that I repeat it here:

"Archangels are superior beings who by tested goodness throughout the ages have earned a place in God's hierarchy. The have dominions which they oversee, and are able at an instant's thought to be there to befriend or smooth the paths of those in their separate domains. God's realm is not a one-man show by any means. He has delegated authority as any good executive would, and as time progresses we will describe these different planes and separations of power. There are superior beings here and there and everywhere, and some of them are able to be seen by earth people on occasion, but don't expect them to come equipped with wings, since we float rather than flap."

Float rather than flap! Surely that line could have been dictated only by Arthur Ford, with his puckish sense of humor.

7

Life-style on Atlantis

During a period of several years, the Guides have made occasional allusions to a lifetime they say that I spent on Atlantis, but not until beginning work on this book did I put the fragments together and discover that not once have they contradicted themselves, altered the names, or varied their information, while gradually adding to it.

My name, they said, was Thelama; my mother was Entreva, and my father Endymius, "who inherited from his ancestors vineyards and orchards protected from the dinosaurs and mammoths by high walls surrounding the estate." They described this as "a compound or village within itself," and said it was located "just outside Poseidon, the principal city of Poseidia which attracted the inventive minds then trying to conceive the Crystal."

Addressing me directly at one point, they wrote, "You who had not previously entered flesh were attracted to the adventure by the challenge of coping with the great beasts then overrunning the earth, and helping the Things to free themselves from their bondage. Your parents you had known before in spirit life. This was not their first entrance into physical being, since they had lived in Lemuria, and because of their experience you chose to enter unto them."

At another time the Guides declared, "In the first physical life that you spent on earth, you were a woman of comely mien, having helped to fashion the pattern for your own shell, or body. The parents had been closely akin to you in spirit, and when you finally made the plunge, so to speak, and decided to try earth living in physical form, they made you welcome; and since giant beasts were roaming Atlantis, you lived within a large compound where the father grew herbs, other vegetables, and fruits.

"It was a happy spot," they continued, "and Atlantis a virtual paradise except for the beasts and the sad lot of the Things. Thus you sought always to help the Things, slipping them extra tidbits of food and gently encouraging them to free themselves from their lowly status through education and medical operations. You taught many of them to read and write, to multiply and divide, and the smaller crystals in use at the time of your entrance were also helping to rid the Things of certain unwanted appendages. Always as a child you were fascinated by the herbs in their natural state, and you loved to experiment with concoctions to ease the suffering of those who were injured by the machinery or hurt in bouts with animals. Thus you grew to young womanhood."

Another time they wrote, "Within the high walls manned by guards were workshops as well as gardens tended by the subhuman Beings who did the heavy farm work, the smelting, and the lumbering, for there were many trees on the estate. These Beings, partly through long neglect of their mental development, would be regarded today as less than half-wits. Some had claws for feet, tails which sometimes caught in the machinery, even beaks instead of mouths; others had feathers, fins, or a rich carpeting of fur over parts of their bodies. Some were docile and others of fiery temperament, so that there were flare-ups from time to time between them and the apelike specimen that oversaw their welfare. The estate was a stone's throw from the great river running through Atlantis which neatly severed Poseidia from the remainder of the continent, and it was indeed a mighty river, rushing and gushing its way from one seacoast to the other. There you played within the walled compound and prayed for the land to be rescued from the giant creatures that were such a terrible hazard to life, although less so on Atlantis than Lemuria, where people were driven to live underground."

I asked about my appearance in those times, and the Guides replied, "Atlanteans all had protruding

noses and sleek hair as black as coal, which they
waxed with honeycomb and attar of roses so that it
shone with a high gloss. Their eyes were nearly as
black, and their lips were often painted with
carnelian or a dye made from the juice of straw-
berries or cherries. The skin was of a ruddy hue,
not too different from some of the American Indians who descended from Atlanteans, and they
sometimes used artificial eyelashes and even eye-
brows to enhance the beauty of their blac' eyes.
It was not the custom to paint fingernails or toenails
during your lifetime there, but people worked various unguents into the hands, face, and upper torso
to keep the skin soft and protect it from the sun.
Since there was no smog in those times, the direct
rays of the sun were unfiltered. For clothing they
wore fabric spun in mills and dipped into dyes for
exotic patterns, and the men were more often pea-
cocks than women about their raiment. All were
garbed similarly in toga-type robes. Sandals were
worn on the feet, and in later days the toenails
were embossed with gold or silver paint made from
the ground-up metals, so that this fashion then spread
to the fingernails. The teeth were pearly white and
did not decay in those days before soft foods and
inadequate diets became common. Then the vegetables were eaten raw, as were the fruits and berries.
Meat was smoked or turned on spits over open
fires, and seldom eaten except on special feast days
set by church fathers or the king. Always there was
a day to worship the sun, and another at the full of

the moon to worship its monthly visitation to the realm of earth as Queen of the Night.

"God was of such supreme mastery that his name was seldom mentioned. He was addressed by a symbol that in today's English language would translate Thee, having both masculine and feminine gender. When it became necessary to write or speak about him, the symbol of a sun with moon at crescent was made, or the lips used to form the sound, so that it became a round O for the sun and a hum for the crescent, or Om."

If true, this would explain the derivation for the mystical incantation "Om" used in meditation.

The Guides said sheep were then considered friends, as dogs are nowadays, and were often kept in the house as companions. They were saddled for children to ride, and were trimmed in exotic patterns somewhat like our poodles, with the shorn wool used to stuff pillows or weave cloth.

"Sometimes the sheep revolted at being treated like playthings," the Guides continued, "snorting disdainfully, but when turned out to pasture, they forgot how to behave with their kind. The rich had great house parties that sometimes continued for weeks, and some were so alluring that guests came from all parts of Atlantis after carrier pigeons brought the invitations and returned with the acceptances. No one ate lamb or pigeon doves in those times, because they were considered to be at least on a par with the Encumbered Souls. The ruling class had open-air palaces stretching for many thousands of feet in every direction, and were as elegant as anything known today. Utilizing pipes, water was easily tapped from wells, and after mountains were formed with the sinking of Lemuria, it was piped down from mountain springs. Refuse was fed downstream into the fast-flowing river that separated Poseidia from the rest of the land. Actually it was not a river, since it divided a continent from sea to sea, but rather like a canal except that nature had formed it. Droppings from the lamb house pets were carefully gathered to fertilize exotic blooms that had been brought from other areas, including Lemuria, and some of these plants formed blossoms several feet wide, due to the perfect climate, the careful cultivation, and fertilization."

Again addressing me directly, they wrote, "During your long life in Atlantis the Great Crystal and aircraft came into being, so that conferences with Lemurians and other peoples began in your lifetime, as did the search for breeding grounds of the beasts. The family into which you were born had ever been of good mien, serving God and lending assistance to others in Atlantis, and you came naturally by your obedience to God and man until you met a person from another area of the continent who had struck out against those divine laws that operate the universe."

Enter the villain! The Guides say that when I met "a young scientist who had come to Poseidia from the far reaches of the continent toward what is now Algeria," I listened eagerly to his tales of the wonders of all Atlantis, but especially to his plans for harnessing the energy of the sun in sufficient quantities to dispatch ships and flying craft around the world. "This greatly excited your fertile imagination," they continued, "and it was easy to fall in love with the young man, but as easy for you also to resist him after you became better acquainted and learned that he accepted no power above his own, no fidelity to a Creator, and seemed to think that he had invented himself."

At a different session they wrote of this arrogant young man: "He was working on a laser-type beam that would project ships into the air and along the surface of the waters, and he considered himself too exceptional in every way to believe that he should bow down to an unseen Being who was said to have created all of the firmament. Thus he revolted against the Law of One (God's law) and influenced others to do likewise. At first you were attracted by his enthusiasm and superior intellect, and seriously considered wedding your life to his, but then his attitudes began to intrude on your peace of mind. He viewed entrapped energy as a source of power not only to operate machines, but also to control the people and even to exterminate those Things who still had vestigial appendages dating from the remote past. These misshapen ones had long attracted your compassion, and you had done much to assist them and try to improve their lot, speaking to them of spirit and of ways to overcome their disabilities. For those with minor afflictions you prepared poultices and herbal mixtures, but the young man laughed at your feeble efforts and said the world would be better rid of them so that they would not reproduce other such monstrosities. Doesn't that sound like some of Hitler's scientists?"

Apparently the Atlanteans knew nothing of sterilization, which would surely have been a more humane way to deal with the problem. In any event, the Guides say the unfeeling attitude of my dashing young beau so repelled me that the engagement was broken, and I went to work in a nearby temple which was attempting to remove some of the appendages through prayer and surgical means. This seemed to blow my opportunities for romance, because they wrote, "Thus you passed your time in service and contemplation, and there was no sharing of that life with a husband."

This sounded to me like a pretty dull life, and I was more than willing to drop the subject, but my editor, Patricia Soliman, who has a more avid curiosity than mine, prodded me to ask for more details about Ruth on Atlantis. Ever obliging, the Guides dipped back into my childhood before proceeding, writing as follows:

"As a little girl you lived in the compound we have mentioned, and since your father was in the service of the government as an adviser to the throne, you went often to Poseidon to see the shining lights and wonderful attractions produced by rays from the crystals. When you were but a child you made trips with your parents to Egypt and Spain, since it was imperative for your father to attend the international conclaves on ridding the world of animals too huge for safety, and also to deal with trade and merchandising, as your father was extremely active in such affairs at that time. At home and abroad you were tutored by scholars of some renown, as it was too far to go back and forth to Poseidon every day, and your mother wished you to be at home with her and the other children, some of whom are with you today.

"As people grew to adulthood in Atlantis, there was little age differential, because all lived hundreds of years. The only time age was noticeable was until schooling was past, since there was little aging beyond the prime, in those golden years on Atlantis. After the age of twenty-two or twenty-three, the principal difference came through wisdom, experience, and judicial attitudes toward others. These people were marvelous in their acknowledged prowess of learning and invention, and such educations as they possessed would now be likened to Renaissance Man who knew something of almost everything under the sun. Different talents were developed, yes; but since this was the first, second, or third lifetime for most Atlanteans, and the first for you, the talents were rather evenly distributed so that each person was able to choose which of his talents to emphasize and develop in that particular life-span. Obviously since lives were long by today's standards, many different talents were selected and brought to impressive advancement, unless the person chose to fritter away his time on social affairs. You were interested in words, then as always, so you did a great deal of writing, and in fact produced a number of manuscripts which may conceivably come to light in excavations at Yucatán or Egypt, although they are not the most important of the documents preserved there. The name Thelama would identify them, if someone is able to break the code and read the language. One that you wrote was called *How to Pray* and was often read in the meeting places where Atlanteans genuflected once to the king and twice to God. Another was called *How to Serve* and described the work awaiting those who decided to enter the temples for communal living, rather than to seek separate establishments for the exclusivity of family life.

"Your hobby was flying in the baskets propelled by smaller crystals, and in these basket-like contraptions you used to drop in on neighbors for many miles around. It was in Poseidon that you met the young scientist at a conclave of people interested in expanding travel to other lands. He was there through his interest in developing the giant Crystal that would permit rapid intercontinental travel by air and beneath the sea, for until the beams from the Great Crystal became harnessed, travel to other lands was tedious by sailing ship. But the revolution was on the way, and with it came all manner of developments, almost as technology exploded in America and Germany in the twentieth century."

The Guides said that my father invited the young scientist to stay at our compound, since he was far from home, adding, "He had a pleasing disposition and engaging manner, and it was inevitable that you should be attracted to him. This was with the full blessing of your parents, brothers, and sisters, for not until the so-called engagement was established did the young man dare confide that he viewed no Creator superior to himself or those about him; that we were natural developments from small beginnings and therefore had no need to pray to a superior Being or to love one another unless we so chose. His view would nowadays be called Darwinian, and he firmly believed that mighty man evolved from algae in the sea that gradually developed over trillions of years into fish, bird, beast, and man. Even the existence of the Manators, those sadly developed monstrosities, seemed to prove his point, for he would nod toward them and say, 'You see, we were once like that, developing from the genes of animals, fish, and fowl. These are typical of our ancestors from which we evolved.' You would have none of this, firmly believing that God was the core of the universe and that he in his wisdom introduced varying forms to inhabit the earth and share his joy, and you would not accept the premise that all came from the same lowly original forms of life. They were each created in their own pattern, you insisted; and the disputes with him became so tumultuous that the engagement was broken, each of you too stubborn to admit any logic in the other's position.

"Thus the young scientist betook himself to Poseidon, where he captured the interest of authorities who permitted him and his followers to work on development of the large Crystal from which would flow the laser-type beams to direct traffic by sea and air. This work took many years and would become more perfected by others, but he became one of the greatest scientists participating in the breakthrough that brought on the successful use of the Great Crystal. This was the beginning of the powerful force created on Atlantis that would eventually destroy that continent and most of its inhabitants."

I asked if the Guides could tell me something more about the giant Crystal, and they wrote, "The secret was in the carbon, for this Crystal was sufficiently powerful to raise the level of energy ten thousand times that of any known instrument today. These souls who directed its construction lived together in a development that had every comfort known to mankind before or since, luxury to such high degree that all of the scientists' energies could be directed to the one project of fashioning a Crystal so skillfully faceted as to collect all solar energy within it and beam it forth to serve mankind. It was a noble goal. With its completion it harnessed so much power that the beams radiating from its central core would drive machines across the heavens and beneath the sea with the rapidity of sound. Thus was the stage set for seeming miracles not yet probed, which will one day return to the intelligence of modern times."

But what in the world did carbon have to do with crystal? Puzzling about this at a later date, I asked for further elucidation and the Guides compounded the mystery by writing: "This was a discovery that carbon as found in diamonds was so piercing in its strength that when directed by the Crystal through the rays of the sun it created sparks of such powerful thrust that ships would take off from the earth and move in air currents, directed by facets of the Crystal in controlled pattern. This was a part of the capstone referred to by Edgar Cayce, for the cap was not crystal but contained these carbon components controlling the energy derived by the Crystal from the sun."

The Guides so greatly relish pointing out my flaws of character in previous lives as well as my present one (see *Companions along the Way*) that I was afraid they would blame me for the terrible Crystal. After all, the young scientist apparently devoted his life to its development after I jilted him. But their jibes were of a different nature. Thelama, I thought, sounded like a particularly nice person until they wrote, "Now as to your life on Atlantis, we would tell you that although you were helpful in easing the lot of the downtrodden, you yourself were addicted to comfort, and when you entered the temple it was with the thought of living well without the pressures of daily life. When you returned to Atlantis in a later incarnation, you were eager to undo that wrongdoing and came as a lowly supplicant for alms, but this was after the second cataclysm and shortly before the earthquake that destroyed Atlantis forever."

Perhaps they sensed my resentment of their eternal criticism, because at a later date they wrote more kindly about my life in the temple: "You entered there and dedicated yourself to developing ways of correcting deformities, and instilling habits of good conduct into children who studied there. This was in no sense a nunnery, for anyone was free to go and come, to marry or produce children, and there were no moral restrictions on cohabitation between the sexes so long as each was of excellent structure physically, mentally, and morally; for strong was the belief that only those with proper endowments should continue to propagate and carry on the race. There were many in those days who chose not to marry and establish separate households, but to live together in these exquisite temples where all was beauty, and dedication to God was the primary function of life. As we have said, age brackets meant little after adulthood was reached, so those who entered there, free to come and go, were attracted to many of the opposite sex even if one might be twenty-five and another two hundred years old. The real difference was in wisdom gained through experience and clear thinking. It was easy to love in this perfect surrounding, and there was no moral onus attached to having many lovers so long as affinity existed. It was not promiscuous lovemaking for the thrill of an evening, but careful selectivity in order to reproduce more beautiful and perfect children. Thus, although you did not wed in that life, you were many times a mother, and some of those whom you produced during that long life are well known to you today and during intervening incarnations, just as are your many brothers and sisters in that lifetime. In the temples of ancient Atlantis women were regarded as the flower of the universe and men as the radial of the sun, so that many songs and poems were written on this theme.

"Atlantis in those days was a model for the rest of the world in all things except philosophy, where Lemuria excelled, but many Atlanteans were philosophical and high-minded in that Golden Age. Curiosity was at an apex and solutions were eagerly sought to all challenges, so that progress was astonishingly rapid. Your mother was a splendid soul who on Lemuria had helped to solve many problems of underground living, and as an astute interpreter of the Law of One she was in effect a priestess. One did not need to remove oneself from other civilized beings in order to serve the faith, and particularly in Atlantis this was considered gauche, for such solitude was a removal of oneself from opportunities to serve, and service was a noble goal. The woman who was your mother then is now someone you hold dear, for she is Hope Ridings Miller (my close friend in Washington, D.C., who is the author of several books). She solved many problems and encouraged you, after the young scientist left, to give yourself to service in the Temple of Harmony not far from the compound where you lived. She thought it a fitting way for one to develop spiritually and mentally, if not tied by strong bonds of love to any particular man whom one could not bear to share with others. Thus, since your heart was not particularly involved with the scientist, you fitted well into the temple life, and your experiments with producing nearly perfect off-spring were then considered normal and laudatory."

And to think that Hope and I nowadays consider ourselves a couple of squares!

Oddly enough, many months elapsed before it occurred to me to ask when I lived on Atlantis, and how I died. On finally doing so, the Guides replied, "You lived on Atlantis more than fifty-one thousand years ago, while Lemuria was still thriving. In that lifetime your motives were high, but there was always some discontent stemming from the fact that it was a first time away from the true world of spirit. This, then, is to be remembered, that a restlessness always pervades your spirit, and a homesickness for that which is spiritual in essence. You departed the body not from physical disability, but through desire to return to the finer life of spirit. When the time drew near for you to leave the Planet Earth, you were ready to go, although not willing to force the day. The mother whom you loved had preceded you, as had several close friends of your youth and middle years. There was no need to tarry, and no need to hasten departure, but sometimes you longed for the serenity of the spirit world that you could vaguely remember, and when a period of calm came, you lay upon your couch and visualized that other world so intently that abruptly you were there, greeting those beloved ones and electing to remain with them, rather than return to physical being. Thus you made your transition peacefully, and with the full right to do so. The convolution that destroyed Lemuria occurred approximately seven hundred years after your soul's withdrawal, when you were three hundred years of age."

Three hundred! But apparently I lacked the perseverance of Methuselah, who reportedly stuck it out in physical body for nine hundred and sixty-nine years, before calling it a day.

On four separate occasions commencing well before I began work on this book, the Guides told me about the Atlantean life of a family I knew then, whom I also know now. Since it is a good example of group karma, the desire of souls who have enjoyed each other in ages past to return again into situations of close proximity, I will include it here, but a brief explanation of current relationships is necessary. Jeanette Longoria is the wife of Octaviano Longoria, a wealthy Mexico City banker and industrialist whose genius has contributed greatly to the expansion of modern Mexico, particularly in the food and cotton industries. Their beautiful white marble mansion atop the highest hill in the Bosques de las Lomas area above Chapultepec Park has been the scene of many international parties, and it features a display of exotic stuffed animals which Octaviano (nicknamed Chito) hunted on African safaris. The Longorias jointly have a five-year-old daughter Jeanette. By her previous marriage to Morris Jaffe, a multimillionaire builder in San Antonio, Texas, Mrs. Longoria has six children: Jenifer, Douglas, Jeffrey, and Jolie Jaffie, Judy (Mrs. Tucker Barnes) and Jana (Mrs. Bernardo Pasquel). The Guides' first mention of the Longoria-Jaffe family began in narrative style: "Once upon a time they lived in a forest clearing on Atlantis, where they dwelt in harmony with each other and those about them. Douglas was an inventor of harpoons and other weapons for survival against giant beasts which then roamed the earth. [He is also an inventor now, although he works in the construction business.] His sister Jenifer was then his wife, and Jana was a doting aunt who helped bring them all together. Chito Longoria was Jana's husband then, and Jeanette was the mother of Douglas and Jeffrey. Little Jeanette (Chito's present daughter) was then his sister. Judy was a daughter of Jana and Chito, and Jolie was her offspring. They were all a closely knit group, a family entity that used intelligence and wit instead of physical brawn to establish their way of life. Chito was especially clever in the diplomacy of that time, dealing with other nations and helping to rid them of destructive animals. Jeanette was like Mother Earth, cultivating herbs and spices."

At another time they wrote, "They were tender and loving, the two most admirable traits. Chito was one of those who went to Lemuria to talk with Elders about the problem of animals overrunning the earth, and he held some conclaves in Africa as well as Atlantis. It is for this reason that he now enjoys big-game hunting, for the success of the Atlantean program helped rid the earth of the giant beasts who had stepped out of their pattern and were encroaching on all other forms of life. (Interestingly, Chito has even stocked his large ranch near the Texas border with wild animals brought from Africa and other countries.) Jeanette loved the flowering things, and was always concocting herbal blends for healing and spiritual growth. There are many anecdotes about her. For instance, when she would create a particular herbal remedy she would want to use it on the entire family, whether they were ailing or not. She called it 'exploration,' and some would rebel against being used as guinea pigs. She was married to the present Morris Jaffe then, and he indulged her in most of her exploits, but would not go along with testing out her remedies hit or miss. She was scientifically inclined in that respect, but it would have been safer to experiment with animals or rodents rather than her family, although all were unscathed. She was her own best guinea pig, and if she felt all right afterward, she would want to try the concoction on the others."

To break into the Guides' narrative at this point, I later read this account to Jenifer Jaffe and asked if her mother has shown any similar interest during this lifetime. "Are you kidding!" she exclaimed. "She has a medicine chest that outdoes a drugstore, and she's always prescribing for us. When we were little she learned to give B_{12} shots and would chase us around the house, sticking in the needle and telling us how much better we would feel. We used to beg her to let us alone, but we had to take her medicines anyway. Once Douglas had a crick in his neck, and he was woozy for several days after Mother mixed up some concoction for him. We dreaded going to the ranch because Mother would pick wild plants outside and make us drink her herbal teas." With a merry laugh, she added, "I think the reason Mother now enjoys living in Mexico City is because she can buy all the medicines she wants without a prescription there." Since all of this was totally unknown to me, I was relieved to find that the Atlantean parallel could not have emerged from my own subconscious.

Months later, after I had completed this part of the manuscript, the Guides suddenly wrote one morning: "So that we are able to fill in the gaps, let's go back to Atlantis and speak of that life of the Jaffes and Longorias. They were so close-knit that when the time came for the children to marry, they automatically selected spouses from among relatives or friends who would live in the compound with them, and take up their duties as members of the group. The one now named Morris Jaffe was the brother of Chito and they had grown up together in the compound, which had been owned for many generations by the family. They were so close as to be of one mind, and when Chito developed his extraordinary talent for diplomacy, the other brother agreed to operate the compound after the passing of their father. When Judy was ready for marriage, she was wed to a cousin who was a son of Morris and Jeanette, and this tie has never been broken, for he is now Tucker Barnes [her present husband]. Morris Jaffe displayed phenomenal talents for handling all arrangements at the compound, and his relations with the workers and the family were so successful that in later years the compound was considered a model for the continent. This was before the sinking of Lemuria and the forming of the mountains, so it is not possible to pinpoint its location in today's geography, except to say that it survived the breaking up of the land in the second of three cataclysms and is not far from the Bahamas, beneath the present sea. The Crystal was not located in the city of Poseidon, understand, but in the environs of today's Bimini Island, where it is reactivating from time to time."

When Judy Jaffe Barnes later read this account, there was a stunned silence before she exclaimed, "So my husband Tucker was then my present mother's son! That explains something to me. A so-called friend had falsely turned me against my mother [Jeanette Longoria], and I had not spoken to her for nearly three years until after I was married. It was Tucker who simply forced me to see her again, and now I absolutely adore her. I'm crazy about Mother, and to think I would have missed this happy relationship except for Tucker! And he was once her son!"

The Guides say the Longoria-Jaffe estate was not far from my father's compound in Atlantis, "but more into the forest," and since timber was plentiful, it was surrounded by wood fencing, with Things posted in lookout towers every few hundred yards to alert those within of approaching danger. It was a vast preserve, and in the unfenced forest areas certain trees were "tied with a woven material that would sound a warning if brushed against by giant beasts." The Guides said I frequently propelled my

"basket-like contraption" to the neighboring compound, and had known the Longorias and Jaffes
throughout my childhood, having accompanied my
father to some of the international conclaves which
he and Chito attended with their families. One day
while there, a fire was raging in an outlying sector
and I helped firefighters cordon it off, "driving out
animals that would have rushed back into the flames
to rescue their young." This led to discovery of a
breeding ground for dinosaurs, which was then eradi-
cated. Concluding their discussion of the Longoria-
Jaffe family, they wrote, "The children were then so
devoted to each other and to the adults that they all
lived together within the compound as one family,
swearing never to be parted."

Certainly today they are an extraordinarily devoted family who seem to have their most enjoyable
times when all are together. Even Jeanette's first
and second husbands (Morris and Chito) are warm
personal friends of many years' standing, and the
families are often together for holidays with Morris'
beautiful second wife, Lisa. Like the Kennedy clan,
who according to the Guides in *A World Beyond*
was also a close-knit group in early England, the
Longoria-Jaffe family had pledged to return together when a means could be found for doing so.
The Kennedys, Jaffes, and Longorias are all Roman
Catholics, a religion that forbids artificial birth
control, and that fact plus the vogue for large
families in recent decades apparently provided the
opportunity.

8

Shift of the Axis

Clouds of impending disaster were hovering over
the earth some fifty thousand years ago, but there
seems to have been plenty of advance warning. The
Guides say that "outer space beings began alerting
earthlings to a coming convolution which they were
able to observe from outside our atmosphere, as gas
belts became active within the cooling landmass.
Fissures were developing that were visible from
outer space, much as satellites now photograph the
movement of storm clouds and hurricanes which
cannot be seen so far in advance by lower flying
planes."

At another time the Guides wrote, "Remember
that in those times the earth was undergoing stresses

as the molten core was cooling. This has been a continuing process. Other erratic gyrations of the earth had been experienced in earlier times, but none had the drastic effect of this one we are about to relate, because previously there were fewer people, the bodies were shadowy in form and able to project themselves to safe areas. Wise men among the Lemurians foretold the cataclysm that was to come, advising those who wished to prolong their stay on Planet Earth to move to safer climes. Some, taking with them their possessions and a collection of vegetables, fruits, and nuts of the varieties husbanded through tens of thousands of years, sailed to Asia, Africa, or parts of America, where they were welcomed by the natives who recognized their superior education and knowledge. Others, feeling that they had had enough of inhabiting flesh, resolved to return to spirit when the cataclysm came."

According to my unseen pen pals, those who emigrated from Lemuria mainly chose to do so in order that their advanced culture would not be lost to future generations and other races. "It was not a mad scramble for personal safety, but a well-reasoned philosophy, that some should preserve the records while others would return to spirit."

Simultaneously spacemen were also warning the Atlanteans of a coming catastrophe, and some heeded the alarm, going to Yucatán or crossing by land bridge and ships to present-day Egypt, Libya, Spain, and Portugal. There they established schools of instruction in letters, mathematics, agriculture, and engineering, and like the Lemurians erected "edifices in pyramidal shape, for always man has looked upward to God."

Apparently the colonists had ample time to establish themselves because the Guides wrote, "In the last days of Mu extending over a few hundred years, there were frequent signs of ominous things to come. The wise priests interpreted these correctly as marking the end of Mu, and increased their warnings that those wishing safety should take shelter elsewhere. The emigrants took with them their knowledge of astronomy, for some had communicated with those from other parts of the galaxy, and understood the revolving of earthlike planets and the whirling particles that made up the Milky Way. New stars were forming and others colliding until they reached natural orbit. Lemurians spread the knowledge of worship of the one Creator in the new colonies, and they helped the natives build temples on which they carved reverent tributes to the Motherland of Mu. In America these temples faced west toward Lemuria, and in Asia east toward the same motherland."

It would seem that this custom continued among descendants of these migratory Lemurians for many millenia thereafter, since several prehistoric temples at Uxmal and elsewhere in Mexico face west, whereas temples at Angkor Wat in Cambodia face east toward vanished Mu. James Churchward, in his Mu series, claims to have deciphered identical symbols on both, which pay tribute to Lemuria. The Guides have repeatedly stressed that there were no language barriers in those long-ago days, despite varying pronunciations in widely separated areas, "and all could readily understand each other, even as New Yorkers comprehend the drawl of Southerners, or Londoners the cockney accent."

Then, in approximately 48,000 B.C. came the awesome event for which the civilized world had long been girding itself. Volcanoes erupted, tremors "violent enough to fold up the land like a crumpled piece of paper" shook the earth, which shifted on its axis, and the sea came "lashing and churning across low-lying Lemuria," so that all except the higher ridges of what are now Hawaii, Tahiti, Polynesia, and a few other islands slipped forever out of view.

"The world's topography was altered in the twinkling of an eye, and for a long time afterward there was a haze over the land that had once harbored many millions of human beings and every type of wildlife," the Guides wrote. "Where flat plains had been were now mountain peaks and valleys. Great Peruvian and Mexican cities, built near sea level, were thrust seven to ten thousand feet toward the heavens, leaving only vestigial artifacts of a noble past. Present-day California, then an eastern coastal area of Lemuria, survived the inundation by attaching itself to new lands (our Western United States) which rose from ocean bed. Rivers that had flowed north turned west or east or south, and vice versa, and the Mississippi, which had once been coastline, now became a mighty river because of the newly formed land to its west. In Africa the Nile that had emptied into the Atlantic changed course with the tilting of the landmass and found its outlet in the Mediterranean. New land appeared in Europe; and the Sahara, once ocean bottom, now became one of the most fertile spots on earth."

And what happened to Atlantis? Not too much, according to the Guides. Some of its western lands sank from sight, and ocean now separated it from Brazil and the east coast of North America. Mountains appeared, and due to the altered position of the equator in relation to the poles, the idyllic temperate climate of Atlantis became more torrid, possibly affecting the character of the people.

I asked about the fate of the huge beasts that had been overrunning the earth, and the Guides responded: "When that which had been torrid became frigid, and that which was one icebound from lack of direct sun became tropical, the dinosaurs, least prepared to adapt themselves to the sudden change of temperature, died by the tens of thousands, for their brains were the size of peanuts before they were shelled, and their great bodies lacked guidance or memory. Thus they smothered, drowned, or sickened from unaccustomed heat and died, as did many of the other great hulks that inhabited the waters, air, and land. Well-preserved remnants of dinosaurs are still being unearthed in your northern regions. It was almost as if God had said, 'Let there be no more outsized creatures,' and there were none. A few giant species have lingered on within the ocean deeps, but their threat to mankind was extinguished by the cataclysm."

The Guides say that although the human population was also decimated by the polar shift, "man is more resourceful than dinosaurs and managed to survive in sufficient numbers to begin the awesome task of reconstruction." Newly emerged lands became available for cultivation, and no longer was there a problem of overpopulation, since the Guides declare that "nearly as many people perished in that convolution as the total population today."

If true, that should answer the question of those who ask how reincarnation can be a fact, when there are more people living today than ever before in history. Our recorded history begins only a few thousand years ago, long after antediluvian times.

Speaking of that long-ago catastrophe that drastically altered the contours of the earth, the Guides observed: "It is an interesting thought that Easter Island, a plateau which had been considered the most sacred area of Lemuria, survived virtually unscathed. Those who had previously migrated to America gradually began rebuilding cities in Mexico and Peru that had also been regarded as sacred because of their temples. Today you will find layer after layer of civilization in the same spots, as subsequent cataclysms ended one era there and commenced another."

It is pertinent at this point to consider the finds by William Niven, a mineralogist who early in this century began excavations in the valley of Mexico. A few miles northwest of Mexico City he unearthed the remains of three prehistoric cities, built one atop another but separated by deposits of boulders, gravel, and sand four to six feet thick. These are types of deposits laid down only by ocean waves, and since the site is now seventy-four hundred feet above sea level, surrounded by still higher mountains, geologists conclude that it once lay near sea level before the mountains were formed. The further fact that Mexico City was an island in the center of a salty lake as recently as the Spanish conquest in 1519 lends further credence to the supposition that it had been near sea level in ages past. From artifacts found at the site of Niven's dig, it is obvious that the ancient people were highly cultured, using iron oxide to cast ornaments out of precious metals tens of thousands of years before the Bronze Age. Frescoes and paintings on the walls of a burial vault predate any that have come to light in Egypt. Among the statuettes and other articles placed around one corpse were green jade beads, and jade is not a Mexican mineral. Was it from Mu or China?

The Guides say the countless millions of souls who lost their physical bodies with the inundation of Mu returned to spirit state, where those who had progressed through helping others were "not required to return to flesh in order again to rejoin the creative force we term God." But others who had sought to exert their will on "whole settlements without heeding the wishes of the inhabitants were scorned by them in the spirit state, and they found it expedient to meditate for a long time before they understood that leadership without consent of the governed is an attempt to play god in human form. When they learned that lesson they returned to suitable vehicles (the bodies of babies) in other parts of the world, including Atlantis, to practice humility and conciliation. Thus we see that as souls in the flesh perish, their real selves continue without interruption, and living today are some who occupied forms in the Lemurian as well as Atlantean culture. Not all souls return at once, or even in a few hundred years, but unless they reach near perfection while challenged by tests of the flesh, they eventually elect to return, to see if they have learned the lessons of patience, love, and compassion."

Obviously the Guides are referring here to karma, the universal law of cause and effect in which we benefit through succeeding incarnations by the good we have done, but must repay in kind the evil we inflicted on others.

The following day the Guides wrote, "When the cataclysm sank Lemuria beneath the sea, the Atlanteans were stunned. They too had regarded Mu as the mother of civilization, even though it had receded in importance as Atlantis rose to the fore. Mu's leaders were philosophers, agronomists, and astronomers who led the world in philosophic and religious erudition, and although overcrowding had rendered the continent a questionable place to live, yet some of its finest scholars and thinkers had preserved the glory of Lemuria even after huge animals wrought such havoc there."

Now the Lemurians were gone, except for those who had migrated to new lands, and with the demise of Mu, Atlantis became the undisputed leader of the world. "The Crystal had served well to spread the gospel of invention throughout the earth, and when Atlantis survived the shifting of the axis, its leaders set about to spread the word of 'achievement for achievement's sake,' which was scarcely in keeping with the older Lemurian philosophy of harmony with universal law. Those who had been excelling in the ranks of technology moved quickly to the forefront, and the new aristocracy became technocrats rather than moral leaders. Science was the new god, and as more and more inventions astounded the civilized world, the people became less interested in God's creations than those by man. This is somewhat like America today, long on invention, mechanical creativity, and a high standard of living, and low on spiritual beliefs and philosophical pursuits."

Rereading these words, I could not help but find the comparison between Atlantis and America a chilling one, particularly since the Guldes agree with Edgar Cayce that Planet Earth will undergo another such polar shift shortly before the end of this century.

9

Mystery of the Sargasso Sea

The Guides are by no means pioneering a new field in their assertion that polar shifts occurred in prehistoric times. *The New Yorker* magazine, in a profile of explorer Maurice Ewing on November 18, 1974, states that "the poles have switched position with some regularity for nearly a billion years—the present extent of the evidence." Dr. Frank Hibben, an archaeologist with the University of New Mexico, says that 171 magnetic reverses of the earth have occurred during the last seventy-six million years. Edgar Cayce and the Guides agree that the continent of Lemuria sank from sight during one of these occasions when the earth shifted on its axis, and that it will happen again. Pythagoras taught the theory of the shifting of the poles in the sixth century before Christ, and attributed the belief to ancient peoples of Egypt and India who also preserved legends of a race of red men who had ruled the world from a continent since submerged. This latter tradition would have referred to Atlantis, home of the Red race, since the Lemurians were Brown.

After the sinking of Lemuria, Atlantis became the world's unchallenged leader, but it was not beloved, according to the Guides, who wrote of its people: "As their arrogance increased, so did their warlike tendencies. As long as Mu held the ascendancy in religion and philosophy it had served as a checkrein on the muscles of Atlantis."

Now the Atlanteans began issuing orders for other lands to come under their dominion, and when resistance was occasionally encountered they took the countries by force. The Guides say that although explosives had not yet come into general usage, the Crystal facets were capable of being directed in such manner that cities at a distance across the waters could be exploded by this force from the sun's rays. Looting became common, and the Atlanteans of this second period took whatever seized their fancy from America, Europe, or Africa.

"Although many Atlanteans sought to maintain the old ways of oneness and love," the Guides wrote, "this new breed reigned for a long time and became so drunk with power that the Crystal was used for controlling the masses. Even the threat of its use against another country often reduced it to submission, and among these were the Iberian peninsula, southern France, and Hibernia, which was considerably larger than Ireland today."

I wanted to know about the form of government on Atlantis, and they said that in the Golden Age "a succession of kings personally oversaw the development of educational facilities and religious observances," but after the sinking of Mu the throne became largely ceremonial, with scientists manipulating the rulers for their own ends.

And what was life like for the Atlanteans? According to the Guides, children were born "with little discomfort" and were taught higher mathematics "almost from kindergarten age." They were cared for by Things who served as nursemaids, seeing their mothers for brief periods only in the afternoons and at bedtime. Rather enigmatically they observed that "there was little regulation of their manners." Schools were held, and "many were the rebellions among Atlantean children who were more interested in inventions than the study of philosophy and grammar." The Atlantean diet included meat as well as vegetables, nuts, and fruits, and the people wore loose-fitting robes with sandals, similar to the dress of Roman days.

"Atlantis was a mighty citadel of learning in those years before the Deluge," the Guides wrote. "Scholars from all parts of the world were admitted without charge to the universities, where they studied such subjects as geology, astronomy, science, calculus, and agronomy. Some were able to compute mentally to eleven digits, and they had a form of the abacus that far excels the computers today. Information was stored in cylinders that were preserved within pyramidal shapes at the proper height, being one-third of the way down from the peak. These cylinders were made of a type of parchment spun from the guts of animals, and were designed to last many thousands of years if carefully and properly stored. Many of these parchment cylinders are now intact in the record chamber buried not far distant from the Great Pyramid of Giza, in the direction of the Sphinx; others in Yucatán are equally well preserved within wrappings of animal skins and metal. We will tell you more about this later. The photographing of the earth was achieved through a process not unlike that used today, with telescopic lenses. Radio was then existent, projecting somewhat in the manner of quartz reacting on metallic substances generated through the Crystal facets."

Life on Atlantis sounded so luxurious that I asked about its money, and the Guides declared: "As to exchange, the Atlanteans used a form of barter at first, in which so many ears of corn were exchanged for so many oranges or manufactured products, but when Atlantis moved into the technological period, dried papyrus was stamped with various decimals to denote value. This was exchanged among the people, with storage vaults holding the actual product that had been placed in security. After the demise of Lemuria, this system was further simplified by the issuance of parchment money, and the government stood back of it, rather as a nation does today. Atlanteans even used this parchment money abroad, for all knew the soundness of the Atlantean form of distribution. Some on Atlantis became so wealthy that there was no place to store stacks of money without deterioration, so the government erected a series of guarded rooms. A fee was assessed for this service, and that is how banking in its most primitive form commenced."

The Guides say that life on Atlantis during this period was "all peaks and valleys—the rich versus the downtrodden Things." These latter beings had few social opportunities and were treated much as India has dealt with its Untouchables for many thousands of years. Some of the Encumbered Souls were high-minded, and others little removed from animals: "For although the souls within were tainted by the Original Sin, and none entered such bodies except those seeking atonement for their original revolt against divine precepts, yet there were glimmerings of hope. Some had risen to higher spiritual levels through devotion to others and willingness to sacrifice in order to atone, not for sins of their parents who had created the misshapen bodies, but for their own participation in earliest times by entering the bodies of animals, birds, or fish, or cohabiting with them."

Then the Guides, in their best professorial manner, made this observation: "Do you understand what we are saying? We do not pay for the sins of our fathers unto the seventh generation, unless we ourselves have in previous lives committed those crimes against universal law. These beings who returned to misshapen bodies were ones who themselves had sinned in a manner to create these imperfect patterns. Thus these Things sometimes willingly volunteered for experimentation with the crystals and surgery, hoping that by removing these impediments from physical body they would free the etheric body and purge the soul. Sometimes it worked, for we mirror our own faults in physical as well as spiritual ways. Many of these souls are living today in normal human bodies, and demonstrating the power of advancement through repayment of karmic indebtedness, although some others are still warped in their thinking and are little higher than the gorillas and cattle from which they partially descended."

With that philosophical aside, the Guides returned to the subject of Atlantis, writing that after the shifting of the axis which rotated the continent more into the Torrid Zone, "some felt that to continue working was too much of a chore, and they became lackadaisical at home while others fought abroad to seize new lands; but this was not hand-to-hand combat so much as direction of beams with explosive potential that could wipe out cities almost instantaneously.

"Atlantis deteriorated during those twenty thousand years after Lemuria to a marked degree," they continued, "and except for its possession of the Great Crystal it would have fallen prey to other nations, since the core was rotten and the excellence was rapidly diminishing. It was the Crystal that commanded respect, and the visitations by Atlantean aircraft and submarines that kept the world on its toes in relation to these warlike people."

But not all nations were supinely accepting subjugation. Arthur Ford and the Guides next told the story of a brave people living in what later became Persia, who sought conferences with their neighbors to resist the aggressive policy of Atlantis. Greeks eagerly attended the conclave, where defensive measures were adopted, and when Atlanteans used Libya as a launching pad for the attack against Greece, they were turned back in a splendid battle. The Atlanteans returned home to gather strength for the next assault, and while there a "horrendous cataclysm occurred that changed the course of history."

Horrendous indeed! The Guides report that Atlantean scientists had been revving up the power of the Crystal to new heights, hoping to subdue Asiatics halfway around the globe, "and on an awesome day they were trying to send its rays directly through the earth to what is now China when the land exploded in a mighty blast, the greatest ever known on earth, and down went whole portions of the Atlantean continent, including the base of the scientific world where stood the mighty Crystal.

"This area is now called the Sargasso Sea," they added, "and is still treacherous at periods when the emission of rays from the Crystal activates with the carbon oxide."

The Sargasso Sea! That mysterious sea within a sea of largely stagnant waters, festooned with floating seaweed, which for hundreds of years has been called "the graveyard of the Atlantic"! Since childhood I have been fascinated by accounts of disappearing ships within its briny deep, and of sailing vessels that avoided it whenever possible because of its deadly calms. Even after ships became motorized, obviating the need for reliance on currents or winds, many still continue to vanish, and more recently airplanes have also been disappearing without a trace while flying above the Sargasso Sea.

Perhaps the most bizarre of these disappearances occurred on the sunny afternoon of December 5, 1945, when a group of five Navy Grumman TBM-3 Avenger torpedo bombers took off on a training flight from their base at Fort Lauderdale, Florida. The planes were manned by five officer pilots and nine enlisted men crew members. In command of the mission, called Flight 19, was Navy Lieutenant Charles C. Taylor, a pilot with over twenty-five hundred hours flying time. Approximately seventy minutes later, after completing their run north of Bimini, a pilot flying above the Fort Lauderdale Naval Air Station began intercepting startling messages from the flight leader. He was lost. Both his compasses were out. He did not know directions . . . had no idea where he was, although he was in radio contact with his accompanying planes which were also equipped with compasses. Could all of those compasses also be performing erratically?

The messages became more garbled, and the station tower was unable to contact any of the fourteen men on the five lost planes. Five hours after takeoff on the routine flight, one of the pilots was heard calling Flight Leader Taylor to ask where they were. No answer. Shortly thereafter a twin-engined Martin Mariner with a crew of thirteen took off from the Banana River Naval Air Station to spot the lost planes and guide them back to base.

No further messages were ever received from the five Grumman planes, or from the Martin Mariner rescue plane. Nor has any trace of them been found to this day, despite one of the most intensive air searches in history involving more than three hundred planes, four destroyers, eighteen Coast Guard vessels, several submarines, hundreds of private planes and boats, plus British planes and ships stationed in the Bahamas. The Navy culminated its inquiry by deciding that "some unexpected and unforeseen development of weather conditions must have intervened." But could this explain how twenty-seven Navy airmen and six planes simply vanished from the face of the earth? Not one oil slick, life raft, or other wreckage was ever found.

Charles Berlitz in *The Bermuda Triangle* defines the Sargasso Sea as an area "extending from 200 miles north of the Greater Antilles up the Florida and Atlantic coasts at a general distance of about 200 miles from land to the vicinity of Cape Hatteras and then out in the Atlantic in the direction of the Iberian Peninsula and Africa up to the North Atlantic Ridge and back again to the Americas."

This sounds eerily like the Guides' boundaries for Atlantis.

The so-called Bermuda Triangle encompasses much of the western part of the Sargasso Sea, including the area where the Crystal once stood, and Berlitz states that within the past quarter-century more than a thousand lives have been lost there, without a single body or piece of flotsam from the vanishing planes or ships ever being found. Some of the planes, he says, have vanished while in normal radio contact with their bases until the very moment of their disappearance, while others have "radioed the most extraordinary messages, implying that they could not get their instruments to function, that their compasses were spinning, that the sky had turned yellow and hazy . . . and that the ocean didn't look right."

Perhaps the Guides are correct in their explanation, but what do they mean by "emission of rays from the Crystal activating with the carbon oxide?" I asked for clarification and they wrote, "We mean that at the depth of the Sargasso Sea lies the mighty Crystal, and at certain periods when the sun and moon are in the right positions the rays reactivate the Crystal, so that it interacts with the encasing carbon, making it a peril for ships and planes at those specific times. A menace to navigation indeed! Within the Crystal lie the secrets that could revolutionize the world, supplying all power needs and energy forces."

Continuing their discussion of the mighty blast, the Guides then wrote, "What remained of Atlantis were two fair-sized islands and a decimated population. There had been no forewarning this time, so tens of thousands perished in an instant."

The Guides agree with Edgar Cayce that the explosion on Atlantis triggered the Biblical flood from which Noah and his family escaped by means of the Ark. When I asked how the two events were linked, they drew an awesome portrait, writing, "The flood occurred when the explosion ripped apart the land in Atlantis, causing storms throughout the Western world, for the tremendous pressure released by the nuclear-type explosion was greater than that at Hiroshima by ten hundred thousand times. Not only did it sink most of the continent, but it caused tidal waves that washed shores thousands of miles away and sent deluges of rain pelting down for several weeks, since it had rent the atmosphere as well as the sea and land.

"This explosion was observed in other planets of our galaxy, and disturbed outer-space beings for hundreds of years thereafter. Such an explosion has never been seen on earth before or since. Flooding was rampant in Europe as well as parts of the Americas and Africa, but largely confined to the Northern and Western hemispheres. Fortunately the beams (from the Crystal) did not penetrate all the way to China through the molten core of earth, but they released such tremendous gases as to stagger the imagination, and for that reason the rains brought down poison as well as water. A frightful situation, hopefully never to be repeated."

One of the most telling arguments for the one-time existence of Atlantis is the widespread tradition of a great Deluge in the literatures of many races, including the Phoenicians, Greeks, Cushites, Chaldeans, Aryans, Egyptians, and American Indians, as well as the Hebrews to whom we owe the Genesis account. Ignatius Donnelly in his book *Atlantis* tells of these remarkably similar legends in splendid detail, so that they need not be recounted here, but his massive evidence points to the fact that the sinking of Atlantis created titanic floods throughout much of the antediluvian world. The Guides say this monumental tragedy occurred approximately thirty thousand years ago and was brought on by "misuse of the Crystal for selfish ends."

One morning before commencing the daily session, I typed out a series of questions: What means of local transportation did the Atlanteans use? Did this continue after the giant Crystal was lost? What was the form of religious observances? I then meditated, and when the automatic typing began, the Guides wrote, "For transportation within Atlantis there were basket-like contraptions propelled by smaller crystals which captured energy from the sun and operated a mechanism no larger than a quart, attached to every basket. They were usually made of wicker woven from plentiful grasses, and would accommodate one to four people, depending on the size of the motors. For shorter distances vehicles were carried on poles by Things, or mounted on their backs. The wheel had not yet been invented, and since horses were not domesticated for working, the streets were free of droppings. All was immaculate. After the mighty Crystal was lost, transportation about the two remaining islands was similar to that described, for many smaller crystals remained in use, but no longer could planes and ships be sent great distances because the power projected by these smaller crystals was too weak."

Now the Atlanteans resorted to windsails like the others, and much of the sea around them was clogged with mud and debris. Many of them "wrangled about their reduced status," while others, "appalled by the evil power of those who had wrought such havoc," migrated elsewhere.

One day the Guides commenced the session by writing, "Let us look at Atlantis in its fading glory after being split into two islands, Poseidia and Og. Atlanteans were still the most erudite and experimental race on the face of the earth, and Atlantis was still the nerve center of the Western world, even though reduced from the pinnacle of power. The intensive training of its citizens in statecraft and geology was a model for the ages. Atlanteans had been forced to take an interest in geology after the earthquakes, floods, and explosions set off by tampering with the gas belts beneath the earth, so a new science of determining ratios of earth strata to atmospheric pressures was born. The geologists were now able to determine well in advance where an earthquake would occur by studying a formula advised for earth pressures versus atmospheric, and 'pi' was invented on Atlantis to determine ratio factors. So-called Arabic numerals were used in

Lemuria and Atlantis, and are vestiges of the most noble system of calculation ever used on the earth plane."

This sounded like gibberish to me, but I include it in the hope that it may possibly make sense to others who are more scientifically inclined.

As to worship, the Guides said that unlike Lemurians who had always "sought God by looking above," in Atlantis ritual was all-important. "A monarchy ruled there in representation of divine power, and the Atlanteans knelt in obeisance at churches. Since they genuflected with one knee to the king, they bent both knees to God in religious worship, and today in Catholic and Episcopal services the worshippers follow the Atlantean custom of praying on their knees. After the second cataclysm people were so disillusioned by weak rulers who had let scientists take command of government that an attempt at elective office was made. Do not view it as persons going to the polls. Rather it was the upper class that in general meetings debated who should be selected to rule with the consent of a board also chosen by the wealthy and powerful."

At another time they wrote, "Greatly reduced now in power and wealth, the remaining Atlanteans tried to make amends, but such harm had been done to the land that much of it was now sterile, as if an atomic bomb had been exploded over it. The radiation dried out the land, so that feeding of the remaining populace was a problem of sizable proportions, and it was at this point that a noble being, Throm, emerged in Egypt to which his ancestors had earlier gone from Atlantis. 'Let us,' Throm said, 'resettle the peoples of the earth where quantities of food exist, and let us all be true citizens of the earth, equally sharing its bounty.' Since the Atlanteans were in worse straits than many other areas at that time, the proposal was accepted, and a mass shifting of populations began, with races intermingling in the Americas, Europe, the Mediterranean area, and Asia.

"Peace descended on the world, and those now empowered to work with the remaining crystals were carefully selected to ensure only the highest motivation. Life on Atlantis became a struggle for survival. Some highly evolved souls returned from the spirit plane to assist in a renewal of faith and harmony, and on reaching adulthood they became leaders of spiritual thought. Some of them went to Egypt and Europe to uplift those Atlanteans who had migrated there, taking with them their advanced learning."

Curiously, modern scholars have been unable to find any evidence of a period when savagery existed in Egypt or India. The former had been colonized by Atlantis and the latter by Lemuria, and it is as if culture sprang full-blown in those ancient lands, having been introduced from abroad. Ignatius Donnelly says ancient Egyptians spoke of their hieroglyphic system of writing not as their own invention, but as "the language of the gods," meaning perhaps the highly civilized Atlanteans who settled there.

Another poser for archaeologists is the absence of a Copper Age in Europe, which should logically have come between the Stone Age and the Bronze Age. Since bronze consists of approximately one part tin and nine parts copper, early civilizations would have known copper before bronze, an alloy created by man. Yet only in Ireland and the Americas have copper implements been unearthed, and the Guides say both of these areas were occupied by the early Atlanteans. Lord Avebury in *Prehistoric Times* (1874) wrote that "the absence of implements made either of copper or tin seems to me to indicate that the art of making bronze was introduced into, not invented in, Europe."

Apparently it was invented in Atlantis.

The Guides say that after the Deluge Atlantis was unable to force its will on others, and some of the excellence resumed as the people once again turned their attention to philosophy. "But Atlantis had no opportunity for recapturing its former supremacy without the Crystal, and none knew how to discover and prepare another such remarkable power source." This, of course, was because outer-space beings had helped in its design. Bickering became intense among those who believed that scientific advancement was everything and those who felt the hand of God in the catastrophe and urged a return to the Law of One. The Guides write of this sad period:

"Philosophy and spirituality had not spared Lemuria from its dire fate, and this gibe was often used by Atlantean scientists to discount the pleas that they would profit by putting religion before science."

Turmoil marked the decline and fall of Atlantis. As scientists continued to work with the crystals, rumblings were heard in the earth beneath the two remaining islands. Many Atlanteans fled for their lives to neighboring countries, and the Guides say of this critical period: "Then came a succession of earthquakes set off by further experimentation which affected the gas pockets and gas belt lying along the Atlantic Ridge that had been formed by the first and second cataclysms. Again it was inventive man tinkering with divine laws that caused the havoc. As the crystals' rays permeated the earth in an accidental stepping-up of power, these gas pockets began to weaken until such pressure built up that explosion was inevitable. Volcanoes erupted in a mighty chorus, spreading tons of lava and belching gases, and Atlantis sank into the sea. Again there were floods in a wide arc that had felt the shattering effect of the earthquakes, and thus ended the mightiest and most advanced technological society ever known to man."

The Guides say this catastrophe occurred approximately twelve thousand years ago, and only a few vestiges like the Azores and the Bahamas survived the sinking. If some aspects of the Atlantean culture seem to parallel today's society, perhaps the explanation lies in a warning sounded several decades ago by Edgar Cayce. The Sage of

Virginia Beach said the souls of Atlanteans who wrought such great destruction were again incarnating in twentieth century America. Have they learned their lesson, or will we again destroy ourselves with our technology?

10

A Prehistoric World-Tour

Other areas of the world were by no means static during the tens of thousands of years in which Lemuria and Atlantis held dominion. The Guides, like accomplished mystery writers who gradually advance the plot by shuffling back and forth between characters, now began bringing us up to date on those cultures.

Taking a long backward step in time, they began: "In the plains of Asia now called the Gobi lived a people who had migrated early from Lemuria while that fair continent still existed as the greatest nation on earth. These descendants of Mu were sturdy, high-minded, and spiritually attuned to cosmic forces. They communicated with the

Motherland through thoughts as well as by ships, and freely intermingled with the Yellow inhabitants who were the original race there. Although less highly developed spiritually than the Lemurians, the natives were a cultured people, quiet and deep thinking, for Amelius and other lighter-than-air souls had also visited there, and the Yellow race had had its Adam."

The Guides said that after the coming of Lemurians, "Philosophy was the favorite subject for children in the Gobi, and a race of Thinkers evolved there long before the Motherland ceased to be. Their temples faced east toward Lemuria, and as in the Motherland the priestly caste withdrew from everyday activities, founding monasteries that have set a record for longevity and culture. After the shifting of the axis that sank Lemuria and raised many mountains throughout the world, these priestly ones set their monasteries on mountaintops, the better to attune to cosmic forces. Thus they took over from Mu the task of preserving philosophic concepts and worship of the true God." Here they seem to be referring to the monasteries of Tibet, whose Himalayas were once a part of the fertile plains of the Gobi country.

The Guides say that because the Great Crystal of Atlantis had been incapable of directing ships or planes to the other side of the globe, only a few Atlanteans at first visited the Gobi and what is now China, but they had "heard of these people with their golden skins and wished to rule over them." Thus, after the disappearance of Mu and the further development of the Crystal, Atlanteans made their abortive, self-destructive attempt to send its laser-like beams directly through the earth to China.

According to the Guides, "the rich and fertile soil of the Gobi" was the site of the first permanent Lemurian establishment beyond the seas. Indeed, the *Encyclopædia Britannica* states that the "great fossil fields" of the Gobi indicate "a change has occurred from a past humid climate to the present desert state, and adds: "Finds have been made of relics representing Eolithic, Upper Paleolithic, Azilian, Neolithic, and Metallic cultures." Churchward in *The Children of Mu,* quotes from Naacal writings preserved in a Tibetan monastery as follows: "The Naacals, 70,000 years ago, brought to the Uighar capital cities copies of the Sacred Inspired Writings of the Motherland." He elaborates: "Legendary history states that the Uighurs from the Motherland [of Mu] made their first settlement in Asia, somewhere on the coast of the Yellow Sea of today. From there they extended themselves inland. Their first exodus was to a flat well-watered plain, the Gobi. After this, records are found of them all through Central Asia to the Caspian Sea."

Naturally I have not seen these writings from which Churchward quotes, but he asserts that both the monastery and the tablets are well known to Oriental scholars and to at least five Europeans who, to his personal knowledge, have visited there.

The Guides say the subcontinent of India was settled somewhat later than the Gobi, because it had been beneath the sea until earlier shiftings of the earth's surfaces elevated it sometime before the drastic shift that sank Lemuria. Since it had no original inhabitants, the brown Lemurians who migrated there in great numbers "regarded it as the first overseas colony exclusively Lemurian," but coexisted with members of the Yellow race who also entered the new land.

"Many priests went there to develop a second Lemurian culture," my unseen informants wrote, "and the Indians of today still reflect the Lemurian countenance despite intermarriage with Black and Aryan races in the eons since. The caste system of India stems from these various strata of civilization: the priestly Lemurians, the occupying Lemurians, the Yellow, Black, and White immigrants, and the Things, who did not physically resemble today's so-called Untouchables, but like them subsisted at the lowest level, thus creating a barrier to a democratization of that society. Since few Atlanteans were then in that part of the world, the culture was not contaminated by their lust for power, but after the sinking of Mu numerous Atlanteans came."

Searching the *Encyclopædia* for any possible substantiation of these assertions, I read that when Aryans invaded India in prehistoric times, "they found it in the possession of peoples whose material civilization was in many respects superior to their own," adding, "It is clear that their presence in India was due to a migration of peoples from the east at an early time." Lemuria lay to the east. Unfortunately our history books cannot delve that deeply into the past, but Churchward says: "Naacal writings in a Tibetan monastery state that the Mayas settled in India over 70,000 years ago and were of a swarthy complexion with dark piercing eyes." This would seem to describe the brown-skinned Lemurians. He further declares, "Like Egypt, there never was a time of savagery in India from which civilization might have developed. India was the pearl on the brow of the Motherland" of Mu.

At this point I should like to emphasize that I read all of these various quotations *after, and not before* the Guides set forth their material, which was new and strange to me.

The Guides next directed their attention to another prehistoric area, declaring that in an arc extending from the Carpathian and Caucasian mountains to Persia lived a White race "who dwelt in isolation from the dark races and drew upon spiritual resources within.

"These were souls who had returned again and again to that particular region, without trying other geographical areas or color, although aware that this endangered their development. Some understood the karmic reasons for assuming different colored skin and experiencing varying climatic conditions, as well as geographical areas, in order to round out their earthly experience. But those insular ones who had lived in the Carpathias several times previously clung to the hope that by returning again and again to the White race with newly acquired skills they might raise that race to eminence, if not predominance."

The Guides were referring, of course, to reincarnation and the need for each of us to experience physical lives in both sexes, all races and major creeds in order to complete the wheel of karma. To continue their narrative:

"Some of these people now volunteered to move westward to the Mediterranean area in order to expand their territory, and at this time many Whites who had earlier settled in Atlantis began fleeing eastward for safety. Since they were not of the Red race predominating in Atlantis, it was easier for them to believe that the adopted homeland could be doomed. Thus these two opposite-moving migrations of Whites converged in the Pyrenees and southern France, where they established harmonious relations and a new culture.

"Simultaneously other Carpathians moved southeastward to Persia, which in those times extended nearly to the Mediterranean, and upon hearing of rich lands along a might river (in today's Africa) they pressed on to stake a claim. Joined by other Whites who made up a large part of the Persian population, they trekked overland rather than sailing by ship, in order to quell any dissidents who might interfere with their plans if left uninformed. Encountering little opposition they at last arrived in what is now Upper Egypt, where they found a Black people of no particular prowess, ruled by a king who was supine and peaceable. With little difficulty they ousted the native king, placed their own Araaraat on the throne, and placated some Atlanteans living there by giving them advisory posts in the new regime."

Rereading this account, I was nonplussed by the Guides' assertion that a White race occupied the ancient kingdom of Persia. I therefore consulted the *Encyclopædia Britannica,* and learned to my surprise that in early historical times the largest area of Persia was inhabited by Indo-Europeans who called themselves Aryans. In Germany many scholars contend that these Aryans, or Indo-Europeans, were tall, fair-haired people with blue eyes, and because of this Nazi Germany laid claim to being Aryan.

To continue the Guides' chronology, they next wrote, "Thus Egypt fell to the White race, and as more and more Atlanteans came for trade and resettlement, they recognized the new ruler, King Araaraat, and agreeably worked with him. A high priest named Ra-Ta, who had made the trek with Araaraat and several hundred others, gave beneficial advice to the natives, who were not many in number, and since some of them were Things who had descended from spirit-mating with animals and birds, Ra-Ta sought to assist in ridding them of their unwelcome appendages. He was a kindly man whose sole interest was in establishing harmonious living and helping those about him. Hearing that Atlanteans were working on the problem of ridding their Things of tails, hooves, horns, and feathers, he went there by ship and established good rapport with the ruler of Poseidia. Surgery was being used, as well as energy from the smaller crystals that had survived the cataclysm, and Ra-Ta advised them of spiritual means that could also be incorporated in the treatment of these conditions. Returning to Egypt he then established a temple devoted solely to improving the physical self, and another for inward beautification and spiritual growth."

Months later it occurred to me to ask for more detailed information about this remarkable process, and the Guides wrote, "The temples founded by Ra-Ta in Egypt were so designed as to admit solar rays without harm. These rays were directed to cubicles where patients stretched out on couches and received the beneficent properties without the dangerous ones. Some were told to meditate in this position while energy flowed through them from outer space, and as this stepped up the solar rays, the patient felt so attuned to the universal laws that all disease fell away, as did some superfluous appendages. There was no thought of disharmony, and as one placed self in this state of being, he was tuned into the divine plan of oneness with mankind and the Creator. This method is still available and will one day be used in the treatment of cancer, for when one is totally attuned to divine forces, there is no possibility of such an affliction. The [cancer] cells that go astray from the normal pattern have reacted with negative forces within the individual, and as they step out of the pattern they inflict disability. If uncontrolled, these out-of-attunement cells will gradually destroy healthy cells and sap the life of the individual. The way to control these misguided cells is to free self of all resentments and anger, cleanse the spirit so that the energies from sun and outer space will reformulate the pattern by energizing the etheric body which directs the healing of the physical one, reestablishing the pattern as designed by that person before entrance into physical being. This will be recognized within the next ten years—that the way to overcome malignancy is to reestablish control in the etheric body through treatment by solar energy. The lost connection between etheric and physical body then reestablishes itself and the diseased cells are flushed off. Attitude, my dear Ruth, is the key to a healthy body, and compassion the fuel for oiling malfunctioning parts. Patience and love, the twin sisters of compassion—the opposites of hatred, malice, and fear."

Unfortunately my Guides are neither physicians nor scientists; otherwise perhaps they could explain this process in more exact details. From my reading in the psychic field I am aware that the etheric body referred to is the aura, sometimes seen clairvoyantly, which surrounds a person from birth and is said to be the perfect pattern from which the physical body was formed. As an example, if one loses a leg it is still there in the etheric body, and some psychic healers are said to utilize that perfect pattern in mending diseased organs of the physical body.

The Guides said that since Edgar Cayce told of the Egyptian period shortly before the final destruction of Atlantis, they would not need to go into detail. "But Ra-Ta, the high priest, was indeed one of the many incarnations of Edgar Cayce," they wrote, "and his son Hugh Lynn Cayce was King Araaraat, the Carpathian whom Ra-Ta helped establish on the ancient throne of Egypt. During this period the Great Pyramid of Giza was begun with the aid of outer-space beings who easily communicated with the high priest and reminded him of the old ways of shifting stones of great weight to other places through visual images and the dissolution of atoms."

At another time they wrote, "In Egypt the White race took over the government, and as Atlanteans were arriving in increasing numbers they at first wanted supremacy, but soon were glad to settle for a peaceful share in the building of a new country, for Atlantis was now so endangered that they had no wish to return there. Earth rumblings and gradual lessening of Atlantis' two remaining islands through sinkings were fraught with peril, and the wise among them were prophesying another inundation. Ra-Ta, or Cayce, was the revered leader in Egypt under the king, and when he decided that a special chamber should be built to preserve the records of imperiled Atlantis, all cooperated in secreting it well below the land surface in the event of earthquakes or deluges. Wise sages from Atlantis cooperated in supplying duplicate sets of histories, and Ra-Ta made several trips to Atlantis to confer with them about preservation of the higher aspects of the Atlantean culture. Identical records were also taken to Yucatán and will one day come to light, revolutionizing the present understanding of earth formation, the creation of life forms, the coming of man, and the governments of Lemuria and Atlantis. But do not visualize these chambers as rooms with four sides, as they are in the upper one-third of small pyramids with vast preservative power. Otherwise the records would long since have disintegrated.

"When the chamber in Egypt was completed, above and slightly to the east of it Hermes began construction of the great pyramid with the advice and cooperation of Ra-Ta and the king. Hermes had been entrusted with the safety of the Atlantean documents and was a towering soul from Lemurian days who had returned in this period of crisis to help salvage that which was best of Atlantis and also seal the secrets of past Lemurian glories."

The Guides said the great pyramid of Cheops was constructed "long before a ruler by that name mounted the Egyptian throne and stole credit for that which had gone before him." Continuing, they wrote, "Ra-Ta was the one who deserves most credit for that mighty landmark. Hermes was the messenger from Atlantis to Egypt and beyond, transporting the secrets to be carved into the bedrock and the measurements of the towering structure. An erudite man, so fleet of mind that he was entrusted with every type of secret since the beginning of time! One of the great souls of that middle period, who had originally visited earth at the time of Amelius and came to be regarded as a god by those who followed him. Spiritual beings had given warning to preserve the records because of the approaching end of Atlantis, and they are still there to be unearthed far beneath the present level of the sand, in a special chamber adjacent to the great pyramid which depicts man's reach for God."

When I later read these words, I determined to

ask the Guides if a "reach for God" was the sole purpose for constructing those ancient pyramidal structures. The next morning they replied, "The original reason was as stated. But since supplies were stored within the pyramids, the Lemurians after a few score years noted the preservative quality in certain sections of the pyramids. Nothing deteriorated or rotted away. Thus these areas were regarded as sacred, and thereafter only the most sacred and precious materials were placed there. The Atlanteans learned of this from the Lemurians and also erected pyramids which became a place for worship above and storage within. In Egypt the Great Pyramid of Giza was the culminating glory, housing every mathematical calculation needed for figuring star range, earth latitude and longitude, the diameter of the earth and the thickness of its molten core, as well as the crust above it. This pyramid was intended also as a storehouse for valuables to be evacuated from sinking Atlantis, but its end came so suddenly that the heritage to be preserved in the pyramid was lost beneath the sea. Fortunately the records had already been buried in the smaller chamber not far from the pyramid's base, where they still exist to this day."

I was aware that scientists behind the Iron Curtain have discovered the preservative powers of a pyramidal shape fashioned to small-scale specifications of the so-called Cheops pyramid, but I was eager to learn whatever else the Guides could tell me about that pyramid itself. They obligingly wrote, "Yes, the great pyramid was built to house secrets since the beginning of time. Its calendar is implanted within the measurements of the steps leading to the so-called King's Chamber, and the Queen's Chamber has the perfect measurements for deciding the times for communication with other planets. The passageways between the two chambers record the ages of man upon the earth and predict the total number of years yet remaining before the revolution on the axis near the close of this century. Other more sophisticated details give the exact location of Giza in relation to the remainder of the world and the planetary system, and until these are interpreted there will be little more to tell. Within a radius of eighty-seven feet will be found the hidden chamber containing the records of Atlantis and Lemuria, so deeply imbedded in the earth as to require tunneling of some forty-eight workers for a year. It is not far from the Sphinx, which was built to demonstrate the work of Atlantcans and Ra-Ta in ridding the human species of animal entanglements, not only the appendages, but the animalistic character of the human race."

The Guides next directed our attention southward, writing, "Now in Ethiopia at the time of which we speak lived one Theopolis, who as a young man had migrated there from Atlantis and attained a high position as adviser to the Black king. He was helping with the transfer of powers from one segment to another, and hearing about the wise Ra-Ta in Egypt, he sent word asking for advice on the transfer. Ra-Ta, with some loyal followers, went to Ethiopia, and after counseling Theopolis remained for some years to establish a system of barter. While there he sought copper needed for the pyramid at Giza, and in that mountainous country was much boric [sic] and copper for burnishing the top of the pyramid. He arranged with the king for a transfer of goods, and on returning to Egypt he found that all was in turmoil due to the landing of many more refugees from Atlantis. After preparing new housing for them, he sent for the copper from Ethiopia, and then instructed the Atlanteans in ways to decorate stone by using burnished copper treated with the borics [boron?], a forgotten process that had preceded the Bronze Age. Now all went well in Egypt until, in a final cataclysm, Atlantis slipped into the sea. We tell you this only to demonstrate the type of world thinking in those prehistoric times and to show the exchange of peoples, ideas, and products."

At the close of that morning session, I was chagrined to read what the Guides had written. I was vaguely aware that Mr. Cayce, in recounting his incarnation as Ra-Ta, had told of an exile period spent in Abyssinia, but so far as I knew he had never mentioned Ethiopia. Since this seemed to confuse the issue, I considered omitting it from the book, but while writing the manuscript decided to consult the *Encyclopædia* in search of a clue. I now confess to abysmal ignorance, for not until I read the words, "Ethiopia is the official name for modern Abyssinia" did I realize that they were one and the same. Thoroughly disgusted with myself, I read on and learned that during the pre-World War II occupation of Ethiopia, the conquering Italians "discovered" copper there—copper that Ra-Ta apparently knew about some twelve thousand years previously. The Guides have an annoying habit of showing up my own stupidity.

Arthur Ford, Lily, and the Group had automatically dated the construction of the Great Pyramid at Giza by saying that it was in progress both before and after the final sinking of Atlantis around 10,000 B.C. Now they agilely leaped backward to pick up the thread of their story, writing, "Let us go to Mesopotamia where an ancient people dwelt in oneness with the Creator. These were Lemurians who had settled there in the period of overcrowding on Mu and were priestly ones as well as workers. Finding the green valley virtually unpeopled fifty-odd thousand years ago, they set to work to make of it a fertile garden, and as the lushness grew, so did their understanding of oneness with all creation. They dwelt in harmony with each other, and since writing materials were at hand in the form of clay tablets sunbaked for hours to harden the writing, they introduced cuneiform to the Middle East. When Lemuria sank, they held high the torch, for not all Lemurian colonies had been so intent on preserving the written language and the religious rites as had this colony, which used the M of Mu to say its own name. These were the first to initiate cuneiform writing on tablets, and except for those areas then above and now below water, these tablets will someday be found. So will the writings of

Atlanteans in different form, in Egypt and beyond. The cuneiform alphabet was so similar to the Lemurian and so valuable in understanding the original writings that it will one day be far more highly prized to scholars than hieroglyphics, or even Latin."

Again I resorted to the trusty *Encyclopædia Britannica* and learned that the origins of cuneiform can be traced back to the fourth millennium B.C. when "Sumerians, a people of unknown ethnic and linguistic affinities inhabited southern Mesopotamia and the region west of the mouth of the Euphrates known as Chaldea." Chaldea? With a tingle of excitement I reviewed the earlier writings of the Guides and confirmed that in relating the first visit of Atlanteans to Lemuria, they said the spacecraft landed "on the lagoon of Chalda." (See chap. IV.) Was it coincidence, or were Lemurians using similar place-names in their colonies? Further historical research disclosed that many words in the Chaldean language of ancient Mesopotamia were identical with those of the Naga-Maya tongue of India, which the Guides say was also settled by Lemurians. To cite a few examples: *kak* for complete, *kin* for daybreak, *ma* for the earth, *ta* for ground or country, *tab* for unite, and *lal* for take.

Since many people assume that civilization has gradually evolved from aborigines with huge jaws and tiny brains, it is well to point out that skeletons of Cro-Magnon man discovered more than a hundred years ago in France prove that a tall people with a skull capacity greater than that of

modern man lived throughout a wide area bordering the Mediterranean fifteen to thirty thousand
years ago, producing cave paintings of high artistic
quality. A popular television series is titled "The
Ascent of Man." Should we actually be speaking
of the Descent of Man? Geoffrey Bibby, in his book
The Testimony of the Spade concerning archaeol-
ogical findings in Europe, says Cro-Magnon man
was not apelike. Rather, "his skull capacity was
above modern man. He was about 6'6" tall with
high forehead, prominent cheek bones and a firm
chin. If he is an ancestor of modern man there
would appear to have been a process of degenera-
tion from that point to the present day."

Next turning to Europe, the Guides said that in
early times Atlanteans settled an area that now
includes the British Isles. "Shrouded at first in fog
and perpetual haze, it had been a good place for
fishing and hunting," They continued, "but as the
earth shifted and Lemuria sank, it developed a
sunny, balmy climate that attracted many more
Atlanteans, for it was then a larger landmass
attached to the continent through Brittany. Previously, little else other than Scandinavia had been
above the sea, but with the shifting of the axis the
remainder of Europe rose and took on somewhat
similar contours to that of the present day."

The Guides claim that the Celts were pure descendants of King Atlas and his offspring—the
original Atlantean ruling class—although after long
intermingling with the Whites of Europe, they retained only the red of the hair and not the deeper

skin tone. The Basques of the Spanish and French Pyrenees likewise descended from Atlanteans, and the Guides say that because of their mountain fastness they preserved the language, customs, and fierce pride to a greater extent than those who more freely intermarried with other races. Certainly the Basques are the most puzzling people of Europe. Anthropologists frankly label them "origin unknown," and their unique language appears to have no common roots with any other known tongue. The Norse were not Atlanteans, but Caucasians who settled there in earliest times, "so that they retain the extremely fair skin, hair and eyes of the pure White race."

"Those Whites who settled in the Mediterranean area intermarried with Atlanteans to such an extent that a blending was achieved, giving them the dark eyes and coloring of Atlanteans with the facial contours of the White race," the Guides continued. "Remember that this was occurring tens of thousands of years ago, so much melding is evident. In Mongolia, breeding with Lemurians altered the pure Yellow strain, and similar intermingling has occurred throughout world history. Even among the blackest of the Blacks of Africa different strains are observed, as some bred with Atlanteans or Lemurians in the remote past. The original race of Blacks had thickly matted hair that might be termed kinky, to provide heavy protection from the sun's rays, whereas some of today's Africans have smooth hair and aquiline features reflecting the Atlantean influence in the distant past."

Australia, they declared, is a remnant of the
Lemurian continent, isolated so long from the world
that the natives became like savages, "having lost
their leaders and priests when the continent sank."
This refers to the Australian Aborigines who, incredibly, were not "discovered" by Europeans until
the late eighteenth century. The nonmountainous,
low-lying land of Australia is indeed reminiscent of
Mu, but what excited me most was to read in the
Encyclopædia, several weeks after the Guides' assertion, that the fundamental doctrines of its Aborigines were "pre-existence of the soul, reincarnation,
and dreaming." Of the latter, "dreaming," the *Encyclopædia* has this to say: "It operated in the past
when the heroes and original ancestors travelled
over the land and left spirit and ritual centers as
they went." Does that not sound like the beliefs of
Lemurians, who long retained their ability to commune with spirits?

One morning the Guides began their dictation by
writing, "Now Antarctica lay in the Temperate
Zone for many millions of years until the shift of
the axis that sank Lemuria, but it was at one time
attached to Australia and in previous cataclysms
had been separated from it by vast ocean, as the
intervening land sank into the sea." Could that conceivably be true? Again I consulted the *Encyclopædia*, and to my delight read, "That a southern
land bridge connecting Australia to the previously
extensive mass of Antarctica existed during the
Permo-Carboniferous period seems to be well au-
thenticated by the findings of geologists." I felt a

glow of pride for the Guides, who imperturbably continued: "Antarctica was known to early Atlanteans and Lemurians, some of whom had occupied it for a time, but the Atlanteans who later mapped it from the air [those Piri Reis maps which we have earlier discussed] found little to attract them there, as it was isolated and overrun with wild beasts. Lemurians tried to establish a colony there after Mu became overcrowded, but found it inhospitable to man, since no attempt had been made to rid it of its dinosaurs and other beasts. When Lemuria went into the sea all beasts perished almost instantly on Antarctica, because the polar shift produced such frigid temperature that none could have survived more than a few minutes."

Thus Antarctica, a continent larger than Australia and Europe (without Russia) combined, clutches its secrets beneath tons of ice, perhaps awaiting the next polar shift to disgorge the carcasses of its once enormous animal population.

The Guides saved until last their updating of the Western Hemisphere, writing, "Let us then go to America where many fled from Atlantis, as had those from Lemuria aeons earlier. This was an agricultural society, and since many were of the priesthood, the crops were distributed equally among those who worked with their hands or their minds. There was then no warring between neighbors. Lemurians had originally occupied the western coast and the Yucatán, but after new lands emerged some of them moved to what is now the Middle West of the United States. There, in loving memory of Mu they built mounds in weird shapes to represent their native symbols, and although they did not inhabit the mounds as their ancestors had done through force of circumstances in Lemuria, these became spiritual centers."

They were speaking, of course, of the Mound Builders, those prehistoric inhabitants of North America who have remained a mystery to modern man. In Adams County, Ohio, is a mound representing a serpent which is 1348 feet long. Other mounds in Wisconsin, Ohio, Indiana, and Tennessee depict birds, reptiles, and animals ranging in height from a few feet to seventy feet, and in diameter from fifteen feet to nearly three hundred feet. Some were used for burial, and a modern study of the skulls indicates that not all were of the same race. Could these mounds indeed be remnants of Lemurian artistry constructed in memory of a time when their ancestors lived underground to avoid destruction by giant dinosaurs, and later because of overpopulation?

Next the Guides addressed the subject of the Maya, those equally mysterious people who have left traces in Central America of the highest civilization in the Western Hemisphere, including a calendar more accurate than that known to Europeans at the time of the Spanish conquistadores. "The Maya," they wrote, "were Lemurians of priestly caste who developed the process of recording time in relation to the stars and outer firmament. The exact calculations required many hundreds of years, as these wise ones intuited the information through meditation and contact with spirit beings, and so long as that record was retained in up-to-date form no wrong would befall the people. That was then their belief, and it explains the precise calculations maintained by the Maya in Yucatán and neighboring areas where other ancient records will yet be found. The Maya purified the strain of homo sapiens with their erudition, sensitivity, and recall of previous life. Always they chose to live apart from other peoples to prevent impurities in the strain and avoid the pitfalls of earthly desires. Those in Yucatán had migrated from Lemuria long before Atlantean perils produced new immigrants from Atlantis, and they withdrew farther into the rain forests to avoid contact with the newcomers. But these Atlanteans coveted their secrets and their grain, and sometimes took from them by force, so that the Maya penetrated ever deeper into Central America, having no wish to fight for their rights. A flawless race, until diseases brought by other races decimated their numbers. Some still reside in the forests, but are so exclusive that contamination with others is avoided at all costs. They are now waiting for the next shift of the axis which will terminate their records and free them from responsibility for the state of the world, for so it is written since the beginning of their calculations hundreds of thousands of years ago. The next shift of the axis will not end the earth, understand, but will cleanse it of the impurities of ages past and mark a new turning point in the evolution of man."

Several weeks later, having discussed numerous other subjects, the Guides abruptly returned to the subject of America, writing, "Let us go to Alaska and the period when it was a tropical clime. For as long as Lemuria existed, Alaska was in the latitude now assigned to Florida, and since it was overrun by large beasts it was a showcase of zoological splendor. Few humans lived there because of the dinosaurs and mammoths, but when the earth turned on its axis, ending the life of those beasts by freezing, a land bridge was formed between it and what is now northeastern Asia, which had also suddenly grown frigid. Thus it was a long time before anyone ventured into that icy region, but when at last nomadic Asian tribes did risk the trek, they were astonished that the land continued on and on, and led downward into temperate regions below the snow line. These Orientals thereafter began moving southward, first in a trickle and then in a flood, finding a bountiful land and streams dancing with fish. Soon they encountered the native Red race, and farther along the Lemurians and Atlanteans who also called this continent home. Thus the Yellow race intermingled with the Red and Brown races, melding the skin tones and producing many subraces; and the reason so many of today's Mexicans have an oriental cast to their features is because of this migration from Siberia to the sunny clime of Central America."

Arthur Ford and the Guides said many Lemurians had earlier settled in what are now Mexico, Bolivia, and Peru, and after the earth shift they reconstructed their cities atop newly formed mountains, "choosing the same sites for religious significance, since the temples and altars had originally been dedicated by saintly Lemurian priests who remembered spirit life and communed with angels.

"Thus they coexisted peaceably with the native inhabitants and with those who came from Atlantis to seek a new way of life after that great continent had been partially split asunder. But with the imminence of the final disaster, the Atlanteans who poured into America were panicky and out of tune with the peaceful continent, and before long they began to betray strains of arrogance in their dominion over the natives."

These were the warlike Atlanteans of the second period who believed that science was god, but the Guides emphasized that not all were of such base character. Some of the later Atlantean emigrants were highly spiritual, and they "brought with them records to be secreted in Yucatán until such time as there was no danger, for none knew what would come to pass in the decades ahead. Thus they built beneath the ground not far from Uxmal a seepproof temple where records of Atlantean civilization and instructions in building a crystal power-center were secreted. But none then living knew how to fashion the long-lost Great Crystal in totality.

"After the final sinking of Atlantis and the resultant flooding of adjacent coastal areas, the site of this record chamber was underwater for so long that those who had known its precise location were powerless to pinpoint it for others, and by the time dry land again emerged none could tell exactly where the storehouse had been buried. Thus it remains for some intrepid scholar at last to hit upon the exact spot near Uxmal and unearth this lode of ancient lore."

With those tantalizing words the Guides concluded their survey of the prehistoric world; and although we have no present means of confirming or disproving it, some geologists believe that our best means of delving into the anthropological and geographical past is through psychic sources.

going elsewhere to live so that they would not be
forced to shed another's blood?

11

Those Biblical Angels

Let us pause at this point to take stock of what has
gone before. It is obvious that the prehistoric world
of which the Guides speak bears little resemblance
to our own, climatically or geographically. They
stress that numerous earth cataclysms have occurred
in the millions of years before and after the advent
of homo sapiens, including many polar shifts.
Modern scientists have concluded that seven hundred thousand years ago the north magnetic pole
was in Antarctica and will eventually return there.
Rocks whose magnetic polarity is the opposite of
the polarity of the earth's field were discovered in
India, France, and Japan between 1855 and 1929.
In the early 1960s the United States Geological Sur-

vey reported on large rock samples gathered from all over the world which demonstrate nine reversals of magnetic polarity at the same times (from radioactive dating) during the past three and a half million years. Even today our magnetic North Pole is not in the same location as the true North Pole.

During the Golden Age of Lemuria and Atlantis, those two great landmasses comprised substantial parts of what are now the Pacific and Atlantic oceans respectively, although they were not occupying the same relative positions in relation to the Northern and Southern hemispheres as today. Little of our American continents and present-day Europe were then above sea level, and mountains were virtually nonexistent until the shifting of the axis that sank Lemuria, folding other lands like a piece of paper crumpled in the hand.

In Alaska gold is mined out of muck that consists of a frozen mass of prehistoric animals and trees, and F. C. Hibben of the University of New Mexico says there is ample evidence that at least some of this was deposited under catastrophic conditions, since mammal remains (a tropical animal) in dismembered condition have been discovered in great heaps. Bodies of other mammoths with flesh, skin, and hair intact have been dug from the frozen ground of northern Siberia, and since the flesh is still edible, it is proof that these great beasts were frozen instantaneously, before putrefaction could have occurred. O. Heer of Zurich published a classical work in the 1860s on the fossil plants of the Arctic, identifying the remains of forests and groves of subtropical plants in an area that is now in continuous polar night six months of the year. Dr. Immanuel Velikovsky in *Earth in Upheaval* reports that in the Arctic Ocean's polar circle there are enormous quantities of mammoths' remains, including rhinoceroses and the bones and tusks of elephants, and he points out that since these members of the elephant family require huge quantities of vegetation to eat every day, they could not possibly have existed in today's climate there, with no vegetation. Obviously Alaska and northern Siberia once were hot. To complicate the mystery, there is scientific evidence that equatorial Brazil and equatorial Africa once were covered by ice several thousand feet thick.

In order to comprehend these startling changes which so drastically altered the climates of different areas, I began toying with a world globe. By revolving it in various directions, and tilting it until Australia lay at the equator, adjoining Antarctica was in the Temperate Zone. The Gobi and Sahara deserts could indeed have been highly fertile regions, since both were removed from frigid areas or burning tropics; and the Arctic Circle, where the remains of dinosaurs, fig and magnolia trees, and tropical coral have been unearthed, came to position in the Tropics.

Thus, if our earth was tilted onto its side some fifty thousand years ago and the Atlanteans did indeed have flying machines, it is easy to see how they could have photographed the contours of Greenland and Antarctica (those ancient Reis maps again) when both were free of ice. Sediment found beneath layers of earth, as well as in ocean deeps, proves that vast areas of our landmasses were once underwater, and an unknown amount of ocean floor was formerly dry land. The Guides describe only three of the countless numbers of cataclysms that our spinning earth has undergone: the sinking of Lemuria around 48,000 B.C., the destruction of a large part of Atlantis in approximately 28,000 B.C., and its final sinking some twelve thousand years ago.

If we accept the word of the Guides and Edgar Cayce that the Biblical flood coincided with the second of those cataclysms thirty thousand years ago, then obviously the Old Testament recounts events of much greater antiquity than historians presently assume. In the nineteenth century Bishop James Ussher packaged all civilization into a neat theological box by declaring that man was created in 4004 B.C., six days after God began work on the entire universe. With modern dating methods, we know that homo sapiens has been striding the earth for several million years, and that our globe is but a flyspeck in the vastness of the cosmos.

The Guides make no claims to the exactness of their dating, repeatedly stressing that earth time has little meaning in the realm of spirit, but with apologies for possible errors they state that "man made his advent on earth (the Adams and Eves) approximately four million years ago, Amelius in light androgynous form several million years earlier, and the Things many millions of years before that."

It is to be hoped that if and when archaeologists dig up the fossiled remains of one of those Things, they will not conclude that it is the "missing link," or common ancestor of homo sapiens and the ape— or bird, or fish.

Until the spades of science began digging into the soil of Asia Minor a century ago, the Old Testament was virtually our only source of knowledge about those ancient peoples and towns. A hundred years later we are still in the nursery stage of archaeology, but with modern dating methods each new discovery seems further to draw back the curtain of time. A University of Pennsylvania expedition uncovered thousands of texts written 5500 years ago at the site of a chief temple of Nippur in Mesopotamia. A half-century ago Leonard Woolley unearthed the remains of seventy-four richly garbed courtesans who lived 4500 years ago in Biblical Ur, the birthplace of Abraham. Skeletons of the women were adorned with headdresses of carnelian, lapis lazuli, silver and gold, cascades of beads and artistic earrings. At a Tell in Palestine the 3200-year-old-skeleton of a Canaanite woman was luxuriously ornamented with five hundred gold and carnelian beads, a silver breastplate, and electrum pins. Within easy reach lay ivory bottles for unguent, an ivory spoon, perfume, cosmetic boxes, and numerous other accouterments in bronze. Do these suggest primitive people at the dawn of Biblical history,

Let us see what the Guides have to say about those colorful characters who enliven the pages of Genesis and Exodus: "The Hebrews were Semites of the Middle East, but according to the akashic records they were originally an admixture of Caucasians with the Lemurians who first came to Asia and Africa during the final warnings to leave their imperiled continent. They had a few hundred years to settle themselves before the final sinking of Mu, but they were homesick, restless, and seeking until they wandered into Asia Minor and found land that would support sheep-raising, for they brought with them from Mu a love of sheep and yak, and knew how to spin yarn." Apparently the yak were left behind in the Gobi country, where they flourished in Tibet after the Himalayas were raised, because no further mention was made of them.

The Guides say that after the demise of Mu, these particular Lemurians became nomadic shepherds wandering through the land, intermingling with the White race, and spreading the gospel of the One God. But some forty thousand years ago, "finding little response to their teachings, they swore among themselves to preserve their ancient heritage by forbidding intermarriage with other tribes who were idolatrous."

Next referring to the Biblical Flood which coincided with the partial destruction of Atlantis thirty thousand years ago, they declared: "Noah had indeed been saved from the resultant waters, but so had countless others, although many thousands did perish in the Middle East, and millions in Atlantis. It was actually Noah who founded the separate Semitic race, and his direct line of descent produced

Abraham, Isaac, Jacob, Joseph, and David, all progenitors of Jesus who became the Christ."

Touching briefly on Abraham's celebrated journey from Ur, the Guides said, "As he passed through Syria the patriarch kept watch over the sheep and other animals in his keeping, and told his faithful followers, 'In such manner the Almighty Yahweh watches over each of us.' On arriving in Canaan he felt a prompting from the spirit world to stop there and look about him. Suddenly a man appeared before him and affirmed, 'This will be the land of your people forevermore.' Abraham in amazement asked how such a thing could be when they had no homeland, and the man, who was actually an angel, told him, 'Thy seed will be planted here, and it will develop into a mighty race.' Abraham, an old man who had no progeny, felt that this was a parable, but in the years to come he indeed sired two sons. The second son seemed to him pure Lemurian, according to the tradition of that great land, and the other such a melding of other races that Abraham felt more drawn to the Lemurian one, who was Isaac. Ishmael, the first son, fathered the Arab nation, and Isaac's seed through his second son Jacob begat the Jewish people. It is important to realize that in those times the land was so harsh that they had to keep moving to feed their sheep and themselves. Thus they roamed, and although Patriarch Abraham by then had vast holdings, yet it was held not by right of primogeniture but by squabbling with others who claimed the land as rightfully their own.

"The Jewish descendants of Abraham were not always a chosen people," the account continued, "but became a special people through their preservation of the Lemurian Law of One and their reverence for the true God. Through this special faith, rather than from piety or helpfulness to their neighbors, they attracted the special attention of the spirit world, which tried to help them in their lonely pursuit of a homeland. Thus angels did occasionally visit certain leaders (prophets) of the wandering Jews and assist in returning them to that promised homeland after the long exile in Egypt. Ever it is thus, that those who preserve the spark and kindle the flame will be helped from the 'other side,' as you term the next stage of eternal life."

According to the Guides, Moses was a Lemurian who reincarnated to the Hebrews in order to help rescue them from Egyptian bondage. "Joseph was also a Lemurian, as were many prophets of Old Testament renown, for they saw the need to protect these faithful ones from the paganism into which so much of the world descended after Atlantis disappeared. Job in a previous life had been an Atlantean who resisted pressures of office by holding fast to the old concept of One God, and when he again met evil ways in Asia Minor he repulsed every opportunity to slander his God. Those Jews who fell astray during the long trek [of Exodus] from Egypt to Canaan were Atlanteans who had also slipped in that previous life—descendants genetically of Lemurians and Caucasians, yes, but reincarnations of Atlanteans who forgot their worship during the period when science was God. They had returned to the Semitic race to undo that karmic stain, and they held firm to their worship of the One God whenever Moses was with them, but stumbled without his constant leadership. Thus it is that we genetically descend from a race we have chosen in order to overcome hurdles and face temptations, although our soul itself knows no racial or geographical strain. In spirit we are androgynous souls without color, race, or creed."

Spirit and soul. For nearly twenty years, since my interest in the psychic fields was first awakened, I had been seeking to learn the difference between "soul" and "spirit." Neither in books nor at seminars could I find a satisfactory explanation, until it occurred to me to ask the Guides. This is their fascinating explanation:

"Soul is personality, ego, the personal *YOU*. Spirit is the force from which we draw our spiritual being, and it may be drawn from various sources both more and less advanced than we would consider our own soul, or ego, to be. When a baby enters as flesh, the soul that decides to occupy that form is one that has through previous incarnations formed a personality and certain patterns of behavior, so that it knows what course it wishes to pursue in the physical life ahead. The spirit then is drawn to that soul, and the soul harmonizes itself with the spirit, or God force, so that it will improve in the path ahead. Everyone would draw only the very highest spirit, if possible, yet each is permitted to use only the etheric spirit that harmonizes with his own stage of spiritual development. Spirit is the essence of God, and although everything in God is perfect, yet the spirit emanations, having been separated in effect from the total whole since man first drew breath, are of varying degrees of order, so that as the soul seeks reunion with the Creator, so also does the spirit essence."

The Guides promised to elaborate on this explanation at another time, and a few days later they wrote, "The soul is the being we know as 'I.' The personality, memories, and uniqueness are the 'I.' It is that which reincarnates again and again until eventually it will hopefully reunite with the Creator as a part of the Divinity. The spirit is the essence of the Creator which is ever present and uplifting. We draw from various places this essence called Spirit, so that when we prepare to reinhabit flesh we draw from this limitless fund of spirit to clothe our being, this etheric substance that resides in and with us and upon which we draw for our spiritual growth. Thus we may be linked with other souls through this same substance of spirit upon which we draw throughout our earthly habitation. It is the essence of God, and the higher stuff of our being. Some call it the oversoul, inspiring us to lift ourselves above mundane physical things and strive for perfection. Jesus called it the Holy Ghost or Holy Spirit, and without it we would revert to animalism in the flesh. Thank God for the spirit!"

Inasmuch as the Guides had insisted that angels appeared in person to Abraham and some other Old Testament personages, I asked for an explanation of the difference among archangels, angels, and guardian angels. Never at a loss for words, they affably discussed each category by turns, beginning, "The archangels of whom we earlier wrote were never incarnated on the physical plane. Not once have they strayed from God's will, and they are so perfectly attuned to his Being that they are as one with him and speak with this authority. They live, Ruth, and are more real than anything you have ever touched, smelled, or glimpsed. They reign over large segments of the firmament and are always on tap for the slightest prayer. They send angels to allay fears and smooth the rocky paths, and although these angels are not winged Beings with floating garments, they are the embodiment of truth and light, and are more real than the souls clothed in flesh around you. Some of these angels have tried earth living, and after blameless lives lived closely with God's wishes have felt no further need to return. They meld with souls in trouble and assist in smoothing off the rough edges. They are there in times of danger and suffering and grief, and are ministering night and day to all who require their services. But it would be better for those in flesh to live according to the precepts of God's word and rely less on angels and their fellowmen, for each of us is a separate entity, a separate planet, and each should be able to complete a physical life cycle without leaning on others and calling so often for help.

"There is a divine path, and once we put our feet upon that path we no longer find ourselves floundering, restless and pleading for someone to pull us from the mire. Find that path through meditation and prayer. 'Know thyself,' as Christ put it. Heed the words of Jesus as transcribed in the New Testament, and heed the truths set down by other great beings who have set the world aflame in their pursuit of God.

"The angels that are called guardian by some people are in actuality the disembodied spirits of those who have been in flesh, and who on this side devote themselves to helping others avoid evil and sudden death. They are good souls of generous nature, although they do not have the supreme advancement of angels and archangels. Some of these so-called guardian angels pass on spiritual knowledge, and ideas for inventions that have been generated here, to those in flesh while in a sleeping or half-waking state. Einstein is a superb example of a Receiving Station who was so attuned to universal laws that he was able during short naps to receive the material dispensed from this side.

"Let us next consider those who unwittingly receive information from this side that may not have been intended specifically for them, such as those receiving plots for novels, or ideas for a needed invention. Many pick up this material simultaneously, as your patent office can attest. These are sensitives who unknowingly are receiving ideas from here that they would merely call inspiration. All are welcome to make use of this material, if it is used for the general welfare and not for malignant purposes."

The Guides then summarized the three categories

of angels, writing, "Archangels are directors of various sections of God's universe, each with assigned tasks to represent the Most High in the day-to-day crises besetting man. Angels are ethereal beings, many of whom have never incarnated into flesh, who assist in the overall design for the advancement of man, beast, fowl, plant, and mineral into a perfect state through their combined efforts. Guardian angels are those who nearly always have been in the flesh and who wish to assist in the advancement of humans still in physical form.

"The Archangel Michael, one of the reigning princes under the Creator, is of such immense value to our understanding of the hierarchy of heaven that we will speak of him at length. He is the brother of the Christ, yet we emphasize that all of us are brothers and fellow creations of God, and although many of us have strayed from the original path of enlightenment, yet are we nearer to God than we are to our own hands and feet and heart. Michael is one of those who never erred, and so important are his functions that he has never been tempted to incarnate in physical form. He stands at the threshold, yet is able to communicate with those who seek God in physical form. He is the tone bearer, as Lucifer once was the light bearer, and Christ the soul of God in human form. Each is necessary to the functioning of a perfect universe, and when Lucifer fell from grace an important gap existed in the Divine plan. Thus sin entered into a flawless plan, and we who would help God to fill that void created by the transgression of Lucifer should weigh carefully our thoughts and actions, so that with all of us combining in good works and loving demeanor, this void will be filled by the body of mankind."

Reading these words after the morning session, I was staggered by the implications. Many of us appeal to God when we are in need of help, but here were the Guides saying that God equally needs our help in overcoming the void left by Lucifer's defection. Apparently they wanted me to absorb this message thoroughly, because three months elapsed before the Guides returned to this subject, writing, "The archangels are not here to rule or direct, but to help those who are in need of the Creator's assurance and goodness, so that if one calls on God the archangels are instantly alerted. Thus the contact is made, and the necessity of intercession is weighed by the archangels. These are magnificent beings, each with his own allotted realm, and because they are the 'think tanks' of our realm, we know them as superior beings. When we face the prospect of an endless succession of lives in the flesh, we realize the importance of becoming more like the angels and archangels, who are so completely aware of God's will that they manifest it automatically at all times and in all places.

"We too would become as angels were we to listen to that still small voice of God which is within each of us, and then turn automatically to it [our conscience] before reaching any decision and making any move. There it is for all of us to hear or feel or sense, yet how often it is ignored while our mind leads us down the primrose path. Here on this side of the open door we automatically know the right move to make, the right thought to think, for we are an essence of God and have no worldly temptations to ensnare us, as do those in physical form. Here we have an awareness of how greatly we have put ourselves out of direct contact with the Creator by willful acts and thoughtless deeds while in the flesh. Thus, instead of enjoying the realm of pure, unselfish love into which we would so happily have been admitted, we remain here to relearn the same lessons we have been taught again and again between earthly lives, while in the spirit realm. See the point, Ruth? Learn it there, and respond to it so automatically that these aeons of atonement and relearning of old lessons are not necessary. Learn it so well that it becomes automatic, like repeating the multiplication tables. Respond so automatically that there is no hesitation between that which is true and that which is false—the right and wrong. Do only that which is helpful and loving, and scorn that which is backhanded and unfeeling."

In their discussion of the hierarchy of heaven, the Guides seemed to have strayed rather far afield from the lot of physical man in the earth. I therefore asked them to fill in the gap between the final sinking of Atlantis around 10,000 B.C. and the beginning of recorded history, and they said there was not too much to tell about that bleak period. "Some descended to near savagery," they lamented, "after the leadership of the two great continents was gone. Transportation again was of a primitive type, and the Atlantic Ocean was virtually unnavigable because of the mud and debris. Floods and earthquakes had destroyed most of the records, and isolated peoples gradually forgot the old ways of reading and writing. Even correct pronunciation and grammatical construction were forgotten as generation after countless generation lacked teaching priests and spiritual leadership. The physical world had drastically altered, and except for a few pockets like India, Egypt, and Peru the people were cut off from the once free-flowing fountains of learning. They became depressed and superstitious, few understanding the purpose for which they were born, or the way to progress. It was a sad age, comparable in some degree to the later Dark Ages of Europe when the curtain was again drawn across education and understanding."

They said the art of manufacturing was also lost, because the secrets pertaining to use of the crystals had never been shared by Atlantis with any other nation. Some of the people remembered how to combine copper with tin to make bronze, but without sophisticated machinery most implements were now fashioned from stone.

"This was the age when animals were domesticated to do the heavy work," they wrote, "because the Things had virtually disappeared, thanks to the success of Atlanteans and Ra-Ta in removing their appendages and controlling breeding, so that fewer and fewer malformations appeared in each succeeding generation. Their disappearance was somewhat similar to the freeing of slaves in the eighteenth and nineteenth centuries, in that a free work force vanished. When men and women were forced to do the manual labor themselves, they found so much work for the hands that there was little time to cultivate the minds. This period is no more interesting to scholars than the Dark Ages of Europe, for people had stopped advancing and were merely marking time, or retrogressing."

The Guides said that after several millenia of this prehistoric Dark Age, "the particularly fortunate blending of ancient Lemurians with Whites in Asia Minor triggered a rebirth in learning. Ancient documents were reexamined, and the cuneiform texts restudied and imitated. Biblos became a seat of learning, as did Athens and other areas bordering the Mediterranean. Egyptians had never quenched the torch, but had hugged it closely to themselves, and when the Biblical people returned to Palestine from Egypt, some of them took a fluttering of that flame. Alexander the Great spread the light of learning with his conquering armies, Athens flared brightly, Rome gradually rose, and then fell. History books record the rest."

Once it was all recorded, but how sparse is our knowledge of those ancient times, thanks to moronic priests who in the name of religion destroyed the tablets so carefully preserved for many millenia in Peru and the Yucatán; who ordered book-burnings during the Middle Ages, and even in fifteenth-century Florence. Sadly, the Guides predict that vast quantities of today's records will similarly vanish when the earth shifts on its axis at the close of this century.

12

Cycles of Rebirth

Human beings, like Cervantes' birds of a feather who flock together, tend to reincarnate in cycles with those they have known in previous earthly sojourns. By some curious law of karmic attraction we return again and again with these perennial companions to work out mutual problems left unresolved, or enjoy each other's company. Nations also acquire karmic indebtedness, which may help to explain the disastrous fall of so many civilizations in ages past. But since each of us earthlings, once caught up in the wheel of karma, must experience physical life in all major creeds and geographical areas, we do not always return to the same race or locale.

Because the Lemurian and Atlantean cultures were of such long duration, flourishing for several millions of years, and because good and evil inevitably exist side by side, it cannot be said that all Lemurians were noble or all Atlanteans sinners. Lucifer, however, seemed to find unusually fertile ground in latter-day Atlantis, which produced a frightening number of individuals who became so enamored of technology that they managed to split apart their continent, and ultimately to destroy it. It is these destructive souls whom Edgar Cayce warned would be returning in great numbers during the mid-twentieth century, apparently attracted to this particular era by the opportunities for scientific advancement.

The Guides, having completed their fireside tour of prehistoric cultures, began a morning session by declaring, "Let us proceed to the next phase of the book, which is the effect of these currents on today's world. Lemurians are rather between cycles at this phase of history, which accounts for our lack of philosophical concepts and our emphasis on materialism and technology. The Renaissance in Europe during the fourteenth and fifteenth centuries, and the American struggle for independence in the eighteenth century, with its Declaration of Independence and remarkable Constitution were primarily the works of Lemurians who reentered physical being to assist at those crucial stages in world thought. Thomas Jefferson, Benjamin Franklin, and George Washington had been Lemurians, and later Atlanteans, so that they were products of both cultures: worldly, astute, and keen on inventions from their Atlantean heritage, but so philosophical and idealistic as to reflect the Lemurian influence rather dramatically. Woodrow Wilson had his first lifetime on Lemuria and was of the priestly caste. In Atlantis he returned as a princeling of the royal house, who early showed interest in scholarly pursuits and church activities. He therefore stepped aside from direct line to the throne so that he could pursue these interests, and he was widely respected as one who sought to enlighten the prehistoric world in philosophy and religious worship; but in the twentieth century he was incapable of forcing his thought on Clemenceau and Lloyd George, who were pragmatic Atlanteans. As we have said, many times these cycles overlap, and some of those living today were both Lemurian and Atlantean, or one or the other. Winston Churchill was pure Atlantean, keen on the strategy of battle and well-grounded in the science of people. Franklin D. Roosevelt was a contemporary of Woodrow Wilson's in Atlantis, when he excelled in statecraft, acting as a liaison between the court and the church fathers in any disagreements regarding worship of God or king. This was during the Golden Age when man's spirit was in the forefront and his reverence deep and everlasting, but in a later Atlantean incarnation FDR was devious and cunning, even though an arbiter. So it goes. Different periods in those long aeons produced different types of Atlanteans. Some were high-minded, and others so scientifically bent as to lack humanity.

"Anwar Sadat was once a high-ranking ruler in early Egypt after the Ra-Ta period, seeking peaceable settlements with warring neighbors. Gerald Ford was a pacifier in ancient Egypt as well as in Atlantis. Always there are some from every culture in the earth simultaneously. It is the preponderance that determines the outlook, and with so many of the middle-period Atlanteans here now, we are sure to have warlike ways, dissension, and inhumanity."

I asked if the Guides could supply details of some person living today who had achieved prominence in that so-called middle period, and they wrote, "Richard M. Nixon had an Atlantean life at the time of the second period, when Lemuria was gone and Atlantis reigned supreme, seeking to control all parts of the earth—not in chains, remember, but in influence—and as a matter of fact it so greatly surpassed most of the earth at that time in what today would be termed 'know-how' in industry, inventiveness, and preeminence in statecraft that there was some reason for it to spread its influence, just as at a much later date Rome had a great deal to offer its captured colonies in law and statecraft.

"Richard Nixon was then a top adviser to the king, and since the kings played second fiddle to the scientists in that period, Nixon was a savvy statesman who wielded influence with the highest scientific minds of the age. He traveled in planes and ships to various parts of the world, even taking ships to China, where he influenced the minds of that area to improve relations and develop harmony with the Western world. He had an uncanny ability to discern what was in the mind of another, and then to speak directly to the point of interest. In this way he became one of the most influential men of the times, and his name then was Rabiosorto. That is a phonetic spelling at best. He lived for several hundred years and influenced his times, in that some areas which would have been attacked by Atlantis were persuaded by him to join peaceably, and although it is not good to subjugate another, nevertheless through peaceable means dignity and national pride were assuaged, and great advances were made in those nations which followed Nixon's suggestion to join hands across the sea with Atlantis. The man was not faulted for his persuasiveness, and although he was what we would term a schemer or plotter, nevertheless his acutely sharp mind simply saw more potential than others, and he did well for his native land. He has had many incarnations since then, but the devious workings of his mind relate to this Atlantean period when he was able more keenly than others to see the opening wedge, the feint and fast footwork, and the goal to be achieved. Who but Richard Nixon at this particular point in American history would have been able to open up relations with Red China, while achieving a working relationship with the Russians and simultaneously holding onto friendship with the late Chiang Kai-shek's Formosa regime. Statesmanship is second nature to Nixon, and it is a pity that those around him were so petty as to entrap him in minor pettifoggery so that, since it seemed so superficial to him with his mind in larger spheres, he stooped to lying to the American people. Watergate was a tragedy, not only for the ugly mark on the Presidency, but also because it blocked further strokes of statecraft which the man Nixon would have performed. Altogether a tragedy of our times."

After this compassionate summation of the Nixon talents the Guides next called our attention to the Orient, declaring that the original settlers of the Gobi were understanding of inner meanings, and full of compassion for their fellow souls on earth. "Thus they left a heritage of blessing in that area which encompasses much of today's China, Tibet and Mongolia, and the deep penetration of spirit into everyday life yielded some of the finest thought yet known—Confucianism and Buddhism."

The land itself may still hold good vibrations stemming from past influences, but the Guides wrote, "The group now in power there is largely composed of reincarnated Atlanteans who settled in the Gobi after Lemuria sank, and sought dictatorship over the Yellow people. Mao Tse-tung is an incarnation of an Atlantean who seized power in the Gobi and held it for a decade, until deposed by Aryan invaders. Chou En-lai was then a native Mongolian who served with Mao and sold out his own people to Atlantean forces. The masses of Chinese today are principally of that period when Atlanteans held sway, although some also had incarnations in the previous Golden Age of Lemurian influence, and as these latter are now beginning to return in greater numbers to rescue China from oppression, watch for a turnaround of that nation in another generation, when these young ones assume power. The same in Mongolia, which has felt the heel of the Russian boot. Returning here now are Lemurians who will resist Soviet interference in the next generation. Atlanteans have been in control of Russia these past decades, although Stalin was originally a Mongolian, bloodthirsty and determined to gain ascendancy by any means at his command, who collaborated with Atlantean invaders of the Gobi."

Shortly after receiving this report, Chinese Premier Chou En-lai died of cancer, and I asked the Guides for information about Hua Kuo-feng, a man little known to the Western world, who was surprisingly named to succeed Premier Chou. They wrote as follows: "Hua Kuo-feng was an Atlantean of the final period when only two large islands remained, a sailor who explored as he went along in surface ships to the Gobi. There he fell in love with a Mongolian woman and brought her back to Atlantis. But she was frightened of the ways of a people who worshiped machines and invention, so she persuaded Hua to go back to the Gobi, where they remained. Hua was not an educated Atlantean, having spent most of his life at sea, but he was thoughtful—one would say crafty—and when he heard that Atlanteans were beginning to leave the homeland in large numbers because of rumblings and earth tremors, he decided to establish a colony, with himself as head, and to recruit all who would come to the Gobi. Then he would set up his own kingdom, with himself as chief, and would rule over that area of today's China that had been raised up from the plains into mountains. Word was sent to Atlantis that all who wished to migrate to the Gobi would be welcomed by their compatriot who had established a colony there for Atlanteans, and many went. But it was an excruciating experience, because he pressed them into service, spying on their doings and so generally harassing them that all who were able to do so went elsewhere, or fled over the mountains into India and neighboring areas. His reign will be equally brief in China now, and after the death of Chairman Mao he will give way to Teng."

I therefore asked about Teng Hsiao-ping who was stripped of the Vice Premiership after Chou's death, and the Guides replied, "Teng was also an Atlantean who showed great diversity of talents. Like Nixon he traveled a great deal in the second period of Atlantean history, often to China, which was a rigorous and lengthy ordeal, since the Great Crystal was inoperative on the other side of Planet Earth and could not accelerate travel there. Teng was often in the Gobi, and since he spoke the language then recognized throughout the earth, he had no difficulty in assisting other nations to remedy backward methods of operation and acquire highly developed skills. He was a pacifier rather than an appeaser, and in this respect he will be good for China and the Western world today, for he has talents carried over from that lifetime when he was often able to sway public opinion to his own views, which in many instances were reasonable and good for those whom he converted to his point of view. Although his power will be of fairly short duration in China, Teng will cooperate with the West to a greater degree than Mao, and will begin the process of returning China to the world of friendly nations. A small measure of capitalism will be restored in China, enough to provide incentive to harvest crops and build farm machinery in particular. Even small private stores will be permitted to operate, and in the long run Chna will become more democratic than Russia. This will occur within the next decade and will tend to deter violence which otherwise would flare in the Far East. China will inevitably become a world leader, although not in the next two decades before the shift of the axis. By this is meant that it will not be considered one of the top two powers until the end of the century, when its tremendous landmass will undergo grave changes and will free the inhabitants from iron-fisted control by the government."

The Guides point out that a rather peaceable breed of Atlanteans who peopled the North African area had "richly endowed minds," and together with the admixture of Whites from the Caucasus area developed the Egyptian culture to a high degree. Of the remainder of the African continent they say, "Not so many Blacks intermarried with other races, and their development consequently lagged behind, but their time will come. Some of today's Negroes are reincarnations of Atlanteans and Lemurians, and this new strain will enrich their cultural development, helping them to find their place in the sun."

They would have left it at that, but several weeks later I asked for more information about the Negroes, who seemed to have been slighted in the lengthy accounts of the four other races. The Guides then wrote, "The Black race began in Africa and was acclimated there through its pigmentation for protection and safety. Although there were some Things there, as well as a large group of Pygmies, they were virtually untreated and simply ceased eventually to be. This was such a paradise for game and every variety of wildfowl that ease of living contributed to the somnolent state of the citizenry. They were happy, contented, and loving, and they rather scorned the strange species of beings who settled along the northern rim of the continent, particularly after the sinking of Lemuria. These peoples were pale in comparison to the natives, and seemed concerned about matters that seemed unimportant to the handsome Blacks, who feasted, reveled, swam, stalked game, and worshiped like happy children on the Sabbath day. To them, these outlanders were an inferior species, since they furrowed their brows about puzzlements and problems, unwilling to let each day produce its own treasures. Of an innately happy nature, unspoiled by pride, the Blacks did not care to mingle with the other races, not through animosity but rather a lack of interest in their problems. They sometimes squabbled among themselves, but seemed impervious to the inroads of other races and were content to live out their lives in worship of sun, moon, stars, and an almighty Being whom they felt reigned above the sun and the rain. Sometimes they intermingled, but usually only of necessity or out of politeness like the king of Abyssinia, that noble being who listened to the advice of Ra-Ta. It was the easy attitude of a people who knew themselves to be superior and did not have to prove it by warlike deeds or showing off. Since the time of their own Adam they had, of course, a spoken language the same as other races, since it was perfect thought communication brought into words, but they made no attempt to record it, and had no literature except by word of mouth, from memory. Who is to say that these people did not excel in affinity for things that mattered? There were few gargantuan creatures, and Africa was not overrun by dinosaurs. The animals were restrained, not overproducing as the dinosaurs and mammoths had done in Lemuria, Atlantis, and other more cultivated areas of the world where the homo sapiens had developed husbandry to a high degree."

To return now to the sequence which I interrupted, the Guides next wrote, "As we have said, the wheel of karma brings back in cycles those who have associated before, and there is no one living today who has not reincarnated a number of times into intervening cultures. None, therefore, is pure Lemurian or pure Atlantean. Some have lived many times in flesh and some less often, but those Atlanteans who have been flocking back in the decades since the early 1940s are particularly influenced by their lives in Atlantis. Many of the Biblical peoples are also back in today's mainstream, fighting to retain control of the land of Canaan [Palestine] since the Balfour Declaration, and those 'old souls' will fight tenaciously for their heritage. Remember that certain past lives are of foremost influence each time we return to work on their particular karmic indebtedness."

This latter statement is in accord with Edgar Cayce, who said certain past incarnations are influencing our present one more than others, and that we can seldom work on the karma from more than two or three lives in a single lifetime. The Guides blame the predominance of middle-period Atlanteans in our present society for the altered social behavior of many youngsters and young adults, with the resultant riotings, kidnappings, bomb-throwing, violence, and drug abuse.

"Atlanteans were extremists," they explain. "Not all! But as a people they tended to extremism and were determined to hold ascendancy over others. They were attracted to return at this particular period by the scientific breakthrough, with its opportunity for their highly developed skills, and also by the permissiveness of today's society. Yet some were so repelled by the violence and aggressiveness of the Atlantean wars that they have refused to enlist or serve in armed forces, finding numerous ways to show their rebellion against established order. These turned on with drugs, joined communes, sought outlet in exotic cultures, or engaged in guerrilla action against the community. This is an age of rebellion and the harbinger of continuing violence through the 1980s, until in the last decade of this century the earth again shifts on its axis. Atlanteans never seem to learn! Another war using atomic weapons can bring about the same conditions that split apart Atlantis, when the stepped-up rays from the Crystal produced megatons of power."

Apparently not all of the draft-card burnings and refusals to serve in the recent Vietnam war are directly traceable to the Atlantean conquests, however, because in *A World Beyond* the Guides said many of these rebellious youngsters were ones who had lost their lives in World War II and, bitterly resentful against the Establishment that had cut them off in the prime of youth, rushed back into physical being too quickly, without taking time for meditation in the spirit plane.

The Guides said there are always some Atlanteans and some Lemurians in the earth simultaneously, because there were so many of them during such long aeons of time—more at one point than the entire world population today. "But the best society is the balanced one when both are present in equal numbers so that philosophy and invention move apace, gentleness balancing overexuberance. Intermingled with today's rioters and troublemakers from Atlantean times are some of the gentlest people in a long span, simple souls who had not incarnated for many hundreds or even thousands of years until this century: the gentle flower children, the nonviolent generation who did not stage protests or burn draft cards, but simply melted away, going elsewhere to live so that they would not be forced to shed another's blood."

As an example of an individual soul who again and again has reached towering heights, the Guides cited Leonardo da Vinci, "a Lemurian who in that continent's finest days was able to reproduce scenes from space visitations and glimpses of immortality, spirit visions, and the faces of his friends." This was in the earlier days before animals became such a problem in Lemuria, "but when he reincarnated it was in Egypt after the Biblical flood, and he created artifacts that are still to be seen in some of the tombs in that remarkably preservative climate. He worked with Hermes on the pyramid, and his fine talents uplifted every form of the life of those people."

Granted that we lack a da Vinci in our hurly-burly twentieth century, I was nonetheless curious to know about the earthly beginnings of some of our well-known figures in the news, the arts, and the professions. Arthur Ford and the Guides affably agreed to check the akashic records, and their first report was on Eleanor Roosevelt "who is once again here between physical lives." In Atlantis, they reported, "she was a reigning lady who passed her time in overseeing servants and setting a social standard for friends and neighbors in an area of Atlantis removed from the principal city of Poseidon. You, Ruth, did not know her then, for she was there before you entered earth life, in the period before the Great Crystal came into being. She was basically a good person and contributed to uplifting those on Atlantis [the Things] who still had vestige appendages from the days of mismating with animals. They were her special interest, and she spent much time with scholars and scientists discussing ways to free these Beings of the unwanted impediments. She was long remembered in Atlantis for her sage advice and willingness to devote her time to these unfortunate ones."

Then, skipping to a different field, the Guides wrote, "Some of today's best writers were Atlanteans in various periods of its development. One was James Michener, who dwelt in Poseidon and attracted a small circle of elite minds to his own inquiring one, in pursuit of the origins of matter and of the human species. He was then prospering as a chemist, and had extended his studies to include all manner of plant and animal life, but was more interested in the human species. For the multitudes of people there was even then no remembrance of creation, and although some would recall parts of that spiritual life when not in flesh, most were as fumbling in perception of spirit as are those in physical body today. Thus experimentation was made with all manner of life forms. To some this was a sport, and to others a deadly pursuit of information to be written into scrolls and preserved for future generations. Sages who could recall snatches of spirit habitation were almost worshiped at this period not too distant from the time in which you lived. All that most scholars had to work with were manuscripts preserved from early days when homo sapiens still had the power to communicate with spirit beings and those from outer space, but these acounts were sometimes viewed as mythology, even as we today disregard the truth in the tales of beings with horns, wings, and fins who once inhabited the earth."

Since I am an inveterate Agatha Christie fan, I next asked about the grand old lady of English suspense novels. To my delight they said that as a small child I knew her, when Agatha was "an old man." This is the way, they recounted it: "Agatha Christie was an Atlantean. It was early on in the development of temple life that she situated herself near the entrance in one of the great arches and began to weave tales of strange sojourns in other lands and mysteries that lay beyond the seas. This was before the Crystal-driven planes and ships came into being, so that her rapt audience drank in thirstily her words of exotic peoples beyond the Pillars of Hercules and west to the Pacific. Agatha was then a man, a seafaring fellow who drew upon marvelous imaginative powers to people her tales with intrigue and inventiveness. When you were a little girl, she was there in the arch of the temple, an elderly and fascinating male who seemed any age, but was actually seven hundred years old. This advanced age had permitted her a great deal of travel to every area of the Atlantic, and even across to Lemuria, although not to the Orient. Arabia was the extent of her travels eastward, and of course Egypt and all parts touching on the Mediterranean. She was so delightful in her ways that this old man became a sort of saint to those who entered the temple, and when his merry laugh rang out, the initiates would say, 'The heavens are rocking with glee.' Agatha has had many lives, in not all of them a storyteller, but this first one so whetted her appetite for the well-told tale and the surprise ending that she has more often than not used this talent in succeeding lives."

I had so longed to meet Agatha Christie that I wondered if I dared mail her a copy of the foregoing, and what her reaction would be. Alas, two days after the Guides gave me this account, I read of her demise. Perhaps the heavens are again "rocking with glee" to have her there in spirit.

The Guides have so often stressed the need for changing our religion, race, and sex in different incarnations that I inquired about several prominent Blacks of our era. They first discussed Barbara Jordan, the outstanding Congresswoman from Houston, Texas, writing, "In a previous life she was a man of substance in the South, an English planter who came to America in Colonial days and amassed immense properties along the Mississippi. A fine, upstanding man who felt deep sympathy for the slaves. But you want to know about her first life, when she was an Egyptian woman working in the Temple of Beauty to assist the Things with their impediments and raise the caliber of physical as well as mental well-being. A classic beauty of the times, and a well-respected woman who assisted Ra-Ta, the former Edgar Cayce, in his work around Thebes."

Martin Luther King, Jr., they said, was a scholar

in Atlantis during the second, warlike period. "He often sailed with foreign delegations to other lands to spread learning, and was well respected for his ability to interpret the laws in serving God and man. Not a famous person then, but a knowledgeable one who knew the man now called Richard Nixon and often assisted him in his foreign missions. In later early sojourns he lived in Rome and in Carthage, and fought well for the ideals then in fashion, and he also had a previous American life as a White man. He is here in spirit now, of course, and following with interest the dissolution of many bonds that had held his friends and neighbors in subservience. "

The death of Paul Robeson during work on this manuscript prompted me to ask about that remarkable man who had a law degree, an extraordinary singing voice, and great acting abilities. It is a sad commentary on our hysterical behavior in the 1950s that his brilliant career was cut short by Joseph McCarthy's Senate committee, which objected to his friendship with the Soviet people. "Paul Robeson?" the Guides began. "There was a prince of a man, filled with multiple talents amassed during many previous lifetimes as scholar, poet, singer, thinker, and a follower of John Calvin [founder of the Presbyterian church] in Europe. He was a Lemurian who hated squabbles and tensions, worshiped the Creator, and awakened talents in those who were then in physical form for the first time. A noble being, who in another life in ancient Egypt helped preserve documents arriving from Atlantis before the final deluge there. He had nobility of spirit and an ever-broadening awareness of the brotherhood of all mankind."

Some readers of my books have complained that the Guides report only on celebrities, and that they seem to have been "important" in previous lives as well. On the first point the fault, if any, is mine. The Guides have told me about scores of others, but since they are unknown to the general public, I have felt that the subject matter would be of insufficient interest to readers of my books. On the latter point, it is logical to assume that outstanding people today have earned their right to prominence by developing many talents in previous lifetimes and making the most of their opportunities. Thus, if we want to be successful in subsequent lives, we should be working now on our abilities, and increasing our potential for growth.

Sometimes I make an exception to the rule, however, when information about the life of an individual contributes to our understanding of the period we are examining. Such a case is that of Thomas E. Barnes, Jr., owner of a lumber company in San Antonio and "believer" in Atlantis for so long as he can remember, about whom the Guides wrote, "In Atlantis he was a man of sterling character, in a situation calling for high business acumen, for he was in charge of marketing the wares of those in outlying areas who had little access to Poseidon and other large cities. This was early in the Golden Age when the baskets and planes operated by the crystals had not yet come into being, and transportation was by sledges where sailing was not feasible. A most difficult transport, since the wheel had not been invented, and either the Things, or a type of buffalo, were hitched to trailers that slid along on the soft soil or sand. Why Atlanteans did not recognize the need for a wheel is beyond our comprehension, since they had such inventive genius, but this was to come much later, and since buffaloes were scarcely domesticated and the Things were afraid of them, it was a fearsome task to deliver supplies where needed. Tommy Barnes as a pragmatist said that since it had to be done, a way would be found, and he worked out a means of exchanging city products for raw material from the countryside, and this exchange system endured for several thousand years. A good man and true."

Discussion of domesticating the buffalo prompted me to ask when dogs and cats became domesticated, and the Guides commented: "Dogs and cats have a long history of devotion to human beings, having evolved from the gentler varieties of wolves and foxes, or tigers, lions and leopards whom man befriended from the larger beasts of range and forest. These were allowed to live within the compounds, where they proved useful in a variety of ways, from alerting to approaching danger to sampling food before being utilized by homo sapiens. These animals, ranging from a few inches in height to larger than man, were bred for companionship, discarding those of more ferocious mien and cultivating those with sunny ways. Some dogs were trained as guardians for children, and others to assist with hunting. Atlantis in its latter days before the cataclysm had begun the practice, and as the Atlanteans set forth to other lands their pets went with them, to the delight of many local rulers who saw the advantage of having animals trained to protect them from their own entourages. Many of those breeds now seen in dog shows evolved from the different uses to which they were put in various areas of the world, from the chows of China to the temple dogs of Thailand and India. Not until man learned how to instill love in others by giving of himself did he attract these creatures to him and becomes worthy of their love. This was actually rather late in time as viewed from this side."

Since my readers often ask if their dogs have souls, I pressed for elaboration, and the Guides replied, "Animals represent families of souls who are a part of the essence of God, although they are not human souls since they are of a different genre, as are plant spirits and tree spirits versus stone and rock spirits and all manner of others, each having his own relationship to the Creator, but never becoming human souls, because all souls of men were originally sparks from God and were created in a single instant. Animals are in a constant state of progression, and as parts of group souls they gradually improve as each member of the group achieves progress. This is a lesson for humans, because although we are endowed with individual souls, yet we progress only as rapidly as we assist others in their upward climb. Animals do not become humans any more than birds or plants become animals, however, for each is a part of a separate kingdom."

The Guides then returned to their discussion of the human species, and at my request described the first physical incarnations for several of today's television personalities. Of Barbara Walters, long-time hostess of NBC's *Today* show who is now with ABC, they wrote, "In the Golden Age of Atlantis she was advanced in her thinking, and so dedicated to the Throne that she refused to join a coalition that would have placed her in a top position to augment scientific studies and discoveries. She rejected personal power in order to serve the king, and one of her many accomplishments was the education of children to be scientific marvels in aerodynamics. She resided in Poseidon, in a villa facing the great rushing river bisecting Poseidia, and there she met with rulers of other lands and envoys from other kingdoms. She later married a son of the king and herself became the mother of a future Atlantean king called Ceres-la-um."

NBC's Johnny Carson, they said, lived in Atlantis at approximately the same time as my own first incarnation, and was "a public figure in those days of entertainment for the masses. The Crystal was used to project pictures throughout the nation, and when he spoke many listened, for he was humorous and full of wisdom. The pictures were viewed on round images which projected as a ray, and were thrown on walls or any blank surface so that there was no need for screens or tubes. His [Carson's] was a unique program in that it combined comment on the state of the nation with play-acting by troupes of players who journeyed about the countryside, so that projecting these pictures directly to the villages and compounds was like extra icing on the cake." This was the Guides' first reference to a form of television on Atlantis, so I was glad that I had asked about Johnny Carson's first life.

Mike Douglas, they said, was also of this early period on Atlantis while Lemuria was still the spiritual leader of the world. Of that popular entertainer on today's tube, they wrote, "Mike Douglas was a delightful addition to any gathering. Full of sparkling wit and debonair manners, he was a politician of great promise who enthralled the public with his terse commentary on the ways of the world. He was of the Golden Age in Atlantis, and having lived for several hundred years as a statesman and adviser to the king, he helped organize a sort of congress where elders gathered to serve in general assemblies. Highly regarded indeed, and except for a slight tendency to poke fun at serious endeavors, he was the darling of the people."

Next discussing Tom Snyder of NBC's *Tomorrow* show the Guides declared: "Tom Snyder drew his prominence in the second period [after the demise of Lemuria] as a well-known raconteur who also displayed forensic abilities, and captured popularity with the masses. Those were the times when planes and ships traveled throughout the Western world through rays of the Crystal, and he was often abroad in other lands staging comedies, skits, and more serious plays, so that his name was on many tongues in foreign lands."

Of TV's Merv Griffin they wrote, "He was in Atlantis as a top politico in the final stages when only two islands remained. He was shrewd in his judgments of people, although inclined to be a bit hasty in his decisions, but oftentimes they were of excellent quality. He was married then to the actress known today as Dinah Shore, who was a lady-in-waiting to the queen, and in their home life all was contentment."

Katharine Hepburn, they said, was one of the queens of Atlantis in the period shortly before the cataclysm that sank Lemuria: "A stately, noble woman whose retinue of attendants worshiped her as a beloved matriarch. In that life she bore many children, some of whom later ascended the throne, but she was so forthright and astute in her views that she was remembered long after many male kings had been forgotten. True to her heritage, she shared domain with her children, as Atlas, the first king, had done, and she so wisely adjudicated their differences that it was indeed a peaceful reign. This was several hundred years before the Crystal was brought into being."

Since she is the most written-about woman in the world today, I naturally asked the Guides about Jacqueline Kennedy Onassis, and they surprised me by declaring, "Jackie Kennedy, in Atlantis during the Golden Age, was a man of some preeminence who was interested in preserving the literature handed down by the earliest savants. He [she] compiled documents and delved into ancient lore of the times when one was able to commune directly with another by thought form. In those days there was a written record of Atlas and his descendants on the throne of Atlantis, and these well-preserved accounts were utilized in teaching children about the 'good old days,' as they were termed."

Switching to the field of medicine, the Guides produced this fascinating account of the earliest careers of today's two outstanding surgeons in the field of heart transplants: Dr. Christian Barnard of South Africa and Dr. Michael De Bakey of Houston, Texas. "Doctors Barnard and De Bakey," they began, "were rivals in Atlantis during the latter days when man was experimenting with the crystals in their treatment of the Things. These two men, although entertaining similar goals, were each trying to outdo the other in their race to defeather, dehorn, and detail the misshapen ones and replace with sections of animal bones or flesh that would protect the openings made by rays of the crystals. Each was lauded for his work, but strangely enough they refused to work together and often labored at cross-purposes. Later Barnard went to Egypt with Ra-Ta and combined some of the surgical work with spiritual means for ridding the Things of unwanted appendages. His was an extraordinarily long life that encompassed several periods, and he revitalized his own body any number of times."

Musing about that strange and wonderful land of Atlantis, where so many of us seem to have had our earthly beginnings, it occurred to me to ask about those two stellar performers, Bing Crosby and Bob Hope. Surely they had left a mark on the lost continent—but to my astonishment the Guides said that neither man had ever set foot on Lemuria or Atlantis. "Bing Crosby, that joyous fellow, was a bard in Italy when there was little of its present shape," they declared, "for it was actually a part of present-day southern France, peopled by the White race from the Caucasus and Atlantis. His life there was rapturous in its quality of living, for he gave joy to all who heard the melodies composed by himself and sung to the accompaniment of a lutelike instrument which he invented and took with him on his travels along the Mediterranean coast. Bob Hope, we find, was with him then as an entertainer of some renown, always seeing the bright side of living, and dedicated to the proposition that so long as men worshiped the one Creator there was no difference in color or manner of living. These two have been attracted to each other in numerous lives since that first one along the northern coast of the Mediterranean arm of the Atlantic Ocean."

And what of those two remarkable women who have headed the governments of Israel and India in our times? Golda Meir, according to the Guides, had her first incarnation in Palestine, "having descended from Atlanteans who went there in early times to colonize and establish a way of life free from domination by those who would seize others' lands by force of arms. This was in the second, warlike period that her ancestors went there, and she herself was boldly assertive in her determination to keep Israel free from further encroachment by Atlanteans. Lemuria was gone, but the world was keenly aware of its great history, and many were also of Lemurian stock in Palestine then. Golda, whose first life was in Palestine, has oft in reincarnations since been fervid in her determination to preserve her own plot of earth, wherever in that particular lifetime it might be. Indira Gandhi originally had a British life in the days when that land was much larger than today, and she was then a man who dwelt in the marketplaces, speaking of the ancient prowess of her people and longing to be a seafarer, as she later became in her long lifetime, often visiting Atlantis and even stepping foot in the Gobi land on one of the long, long voyages by sailing ship."

Before leaving the subject of individual beginnings in the earth, I had another question to ask. What of those great lovers, Liz and Richard, who have monopolized the world's center stage during the past decade, and are once more separated? The Guides duly searched the akashic records and reported as follows: "Elizabeth Taylor and Richard Burton, so off again, on again as to reflect their many karmic ties! In Atlantis their roles were reversed, she the man and he the woman, and through countless ages they have fought and loved again, but inevitably have returned to each other. In this present life they will scarcely experience supreme happiness, but in Atlantis they swore to find each other again and again. They were strongly influenced by the church, and although they had entered temple life in the Golden Age, even as you did, Ruth, on finding each other they foreswore other lovers to withdraw to family life, not in busy Poseidon but in the countryside, and statecraft was their primary interest aside from gardening and herbal mixtures. They have been together in other incarnations since, in Egypt, in Palestine, in Athens, in Rome, and in seventeenth-century France, and unless they resolve their mutual problems in this lifetime they will have continuing entanglements with each other as well as others of the opposite sex in future lives to come. Why has it been so difficult for them to find harmonious living? Because each has an ego that blunts the other's, and until one finds the grace to say, 'You are the greater and I the lesser,' this love-hate relationship is doomed to be replayed on the stages of innumerable worlds to come."

Having disposed of my specific questions, the Guides then drew a parallel between the United States and prehistoric Atlantis, saying that when the fledgling United States opened the floodgates to all peoples and became a melting pot for the poor of every nation, race, and creed we became strong. "Until this century, the U.S. was a splendid example of what Atlantis had been in its Golden Ages when every race was welcomed there, and all were striving to progress spiritually, mentally, and culturally," they said.

Then they delivered this lecture: "The United States is so similar to Atlantis in so many ways that surely a parallel is to be drawn between the aspects that were great and those that led to the downfall of that mighty land. Surely we will curb our insatiable quest for technological weapons of war and leadership of the world, for as we live rightly and lend a helping hand when necessary we are serving the purpose of our creation, but not when we intervene militarily even to protect weaker nations. If they should go Communist they at least will live, and sometime will again emerge as a free people with lessons learned. Stay out of the world power-struggles and away from the shaking fist. Concentrate on America's opportunity to set such a high standard of morals, democracy, freedom, and opportunity that all will wish of their own accord to follow this example. Might never makes Right, so our veiled fist serves little purpose and we made of Vietnam a graveyard for the hopes of those people who were caught in the eternal conflict between good and evil. After years of bloodshed and hardship, the ones you fought against have had their way, so what was the fighting all about? Step aside and let others defend their own precepts, while setting a moral tone and becoming an object lesson for others of the world. The present path is leading straight to another struggle in the eighties and early nineties, before the holocaust releases gases of such velocity as to speed the turn on the axis."

Disturbed, I asked if such a catastrophe could be avoided, and they replied, "We are unable to say because it is there, around the bend in the river, and to us on this side it would seem inevitable. Often, however, there is grace for people when humbly sought, so why not for nations and puny planets such as earth?" Their reference here was apparently to Edgar Cayce's dictum that the law of grace supersedes the law of karma. But if I correctly interpret what has been written, the Guides are implying that unless Divine grace is dispensed, we face twenty more years of squabbling, violence, bloodshed, and perhaps even a nuclear war before the earth again shifts on its axis at the close of the century. Thereafter, a "race of pacifists" now being born will take control and usher in a new era of peace and reconstruction.

The Piscean Age now drawing to a close after some two thousand years has seen so much strife that I asked the Guides for comment on the Aquarian Age we are entering. This was their reply: "The earth turns in such a way that, like souls inhabiting human bodies, it is influenced by the signs of the zodiacs, the pull of the moon, and the influence of the galaxy. Thus when it enters a new zodiacal sign, it too reflects the vibrations of that period. As this Aquarian Age begins, the minds of men will be opened to the reality of communication between the two so-called worlds, for it is all one world inhabited by those in flesh and those in spirit. As we attune ourselves to the new influences of this age, following the Piscean Age that knew Jesus in the flesh, earth people will be able to open their eyes to those in spirit form and sense the reality of what we tell you: that those in spirit are more alive than those in flesh, since their senses are unimpeded by barriers as yours are now. And those spirits can disclose the natural laws of the universe which have been open to man always, but untapped and unrealized. Thus in this new age we will manifest and be seen as well as heard by those whose minds are open to the realities of this natural law."

If this should indeed come to pass in the coming decades, presumably many of us now in flesh will be spirits then, and no doubt clamoring to be heard by those we left behind.

13

Planetary Visits

If we accept the premise of countless astrologers that humans, plants, animals, and even fish and fowl are affected by planetary influences, it is logical to assume that the earth itself is similarly swayed. All of us are aware of ocean tides caused by the attraction of the moon and the sun, and since time immemorial farmers have been planting crops at particular stages of the moon. But the Guides now take us a giant step forward by asserting that between lives it is also necessary to experience the vibrations of other planets before completing our spiritual development and reuniting with the Creator.

Arthur Ford and the Guides touched lightly on

this subject in the materials they dictated for *A World Beyond*, but in preparing for this manuscript they went into considerably more detail. After briefly reviewing what they said in that book about the necessity for meditation even after physical death, and the ability of those in spirit form to be anywhere on earth simply by wishing themselves there, they declared that sooner or later a soul will feel the urge to enter other realms of the spirit and undergo the influence of various planets.

"To experience this novelty we venture onward and outward," they began, "willing ourselves to be in the area of Mars or Neptune or Uranus, for instance. First we 'think' ourselves there. Then we are as pinpoints of light which pierce the gloom, and before we know it we are there on the surface, let us say, of Mars. Whether we actually are there or whether it is an altered state of consciousness is difficult to say, because of the fact that we are anywhere at any time we choose to be on earth. When we do the same with other planets, we are gravely affected by their influence but not, of course, by their climate or lack of climate. We are there as a spirit rather than a physical being, and until we have weathered those storms of the spirit, we are unable to progress to other spheres. Some are less difficult than others to withstand, and if the soul senses himself to be rather underdeveloped, he may choose to go first to one of the softer states of consciousness such as Venus, where love rules and one is eventually shorn of his feelings of frustration, irritation, disharmonious thought, and sinful ways.

"When the soul elects to move forward in consciousness to the influence of Venus, he may at first seem out of place, because there are no other souls with like interests. Those souls who are perfecting their natures in Venus light are gentle, loving, and filled with adoration for the Creator and each other. Thus it seems at first like moving into a children's nursery, or more aptly into an asylum where only the gentlest of retarded adults are contained in happy togetherness. The atmosphere is gentle beyond belief, and it is therefore a shock to those souls still involved in earth's activities, who have not yet shed their concern for worldly challenges and loved ones still in flesh. Jesus said we would need to give up our families and follow him to reach salvation, and it was of the Venus period that he spoke. Venus is a form of perfect love, and woe be to those who take their enmities with them there, for so cloying is the atmosphere that if one has not shed his fears and dislikes by the time he reaches Venus, he finds himself submerged in such softness and sweetness that he frantically struggles for something substantial. This atmosphere is so difficult for some that they elect to return to the state where we [the Guides] are now, and even to reincarnate, for they find it too wrenching to live in a state of pure shining love. This is why, from counselors here, we learn that gentle Venus is not for everyone the best first choice in the path of progression."

The Guides said that some, after concluding that they are not ready for Venus, may decide to pass to Mars, "where in that harsh and simmering atmosphere they may burn off their fiery tempers and warlike manner, for to rage and flame in the Mars atmosphere is unbelievably difficult because of its violent nature. In Mars we pit ourselves against the dislikes that others have for us, and if we return this in kind, it becomes a test of all that is worst in human nature since the beginning of homo sapiens on earth. Best to mend one's fences while in physical life, and through devotion heal animosities that we have inspired in others, for to meet this in the atmosphere of Mars is a shattering experience. The pressure on our souls is almost unbearable at first, because it seems like a vortex of storms and turbulent thought. It is no place to linger if one loves peace and harmony, but is necessary, before we can advance, to learn to withstand the buffeting and turmoil and replace its storm with calm and tranquil thoughts. It is a hard lesson but one which, having been withstood, curbs the anger and warlike feelings within a soul, cleansing it for the next stage of development. For those who are able to endure the oppressive influence of Mars, the burning off is rapid and the stay is not prolonged, but so many are frightened by it that they return here quickly to try a different state of consciousness. They may next choose Uranus, the one which proved so difficult for Arthur that we will discuss it tomorrow."

Difficult for Arthur Ford! How well I remembered, with a shiver of apprehension, Arthur's assertion in *A World Beyond* that he had visited three planets between previous earth lives, and might decide to continue that cycle soon, adding, "But this I know: I do not want to visit Uranus again." What, I wondered, is so terrible about Uranus?

True to their promise, the Guides began the next day's session by writing, "Now we will discuss Uranus. Here is the influence of truce, truce, truce, where many souls have learned to settle all by simply swearing not to recognize the conditions that caused a situation in the first place. By 'truce' is not meant carefully mapping out a strategy to solve a given problem, but simply not settling it at all. To take an example, whereas Dr. Kissinger hassled with Egyptian and Israeli leaders over agreements for a common ground to end their disputes, in Uranus all issues are simply ignored, and the warring souls look the other way until the problem goes away. But this is not as easy as it sounds, for bottled up within them are all the resentment, flaming fury, and indignation of a lifetime in flesh; and rather than settling the issue, in Uranus it is so completely ignored that after a long period of time it drains off from the spiritual body like stagnated [*sic*] pus from a physical one. It is an ordeal to endure this Uranus period, particularly for those who feel justified in their bitter resentment against others who have wronged them, but if they are able to stick it out long enough, the poison does eventually drain away. Sometimes, instead of enduring this lengthy waiting period, the souls most tormented by this laissez-faire attitude will rush back into physical bodies at the first opportunity, determined to resolve the problem in earthly bodies where combat or peaceful negotiations are available.

"The influence of Neptune is more beneficent than Mars or Uranus by far. Here the gentler sway of passions leads to tranquility of soul and the deepest of restful growth. Here we have such a benevolent state that many are tempted to dwell too long, but those who are eager to press on to ultimate reunion with the Creator know better than to tarry when states are too tranquil, because hard challenges provide opportunity for faster spiritual growth. After completing a period in Neptune, one is ready for such severe challenges as that of Uranus, which torments us with deeds left undone and conflicts left unresolved in each life. Uranus hones the soul.

At another time the Guides volunteered: "Now let us speak of Jupiter, that towering planet whose influence is so keenly felt on the earth plane. Jupiter teaches restraint at the same time that it builds firm determination for the Right. It is benign in influence and strictly in accord with that which is righteous in man's nature. But at the same time it permits no ego, and whenever man's desires and feelings of superiority take the ascendancy, Jupiter acts as an umbilical cord to remind that man is but a puny thing, dependent on a mother who brought him forth in pain. Jupiter is an ascendant, serving as the Mother and Father Creator in One. It remorselessly rebukes those who think to dominate another, and has patience only for the meek, who shall inherit the earth. Here the ego meets its greater match, and here it is that the soul must shed its feeling that because of remarkable differences within self he is superior and more ready than others for reunion with God. Those blessed Disciples who expected to sit on the right and left hand of Jesus in the throne of heaven spent some little time under the influence of Jupiter, for although they had been chosen by the Son of God as Disciples, they found it necessary to pay back for their assumption that they were therefore above mortal men."

This illustration presumably refers to the New Testament account (Matt. 20:20–29) in which the mother of James and John asked Jesus to grant permission for her two sons to sit on each side of him in his kingdom, and Jesus replied that only God could make that choice.

I asked the Guides if we are influenced by stars other than those in our zodiac, and they cryptically replied, "Since we are earthlings we are concerned primarily with our own planetary system, although it is possible to pass beyond it for smoothing off rough edges of our character. Arcturus is an interesting example of a star which has a decided effect on our spiritual growth, for those who visit Arcturus between physical lives find a similar situation to our own, except that the life form is different there: rock formations of tremendous vibratory capacity and some plant life, although not of the type we would recognize. Perhaps it is the beginning of growth form, although as yet it is a barren land as far as earthlings are concerned. There we occupy no space, but as we feel our way along in spirit we encounter tremendous hurdles of a type unknown in earthly physical being—wind pressures and barriers so real as to be dealt with only through acts of forcefulness, a strengthening of one's determination, and a melding of that which is good in various other forms. This is almost impossible to explain in terms you would understand."

During a period of several years, the Guides had occasionally supplied material about five of the planets in our own system, but I had to prompt them for information about Mercury, Saturn, and Pluto. After doing so, they wrote, "Mercury is of quicksilver. Mercury is where one is able to review flashbacks of all preceding lives and assess the upward or downward direction of one's activities. A good place to recast and reframe one's motives and determine to find something of value in each incarnation on which to build for a supreme effort to erase all bad karma in a single lifetime. Mercury is a necessary step in the evolution of our spiritual being, and because of its low key it is valuable, but do not view this as an easy Rest Stop, for to face oneself and review all the mistakes and sins of an entire evolutionary process is rather torturous. Stop now to review everything you've done in his particular lifetime of which you are not proud, and which you would not wish another to know. Multiply this by many thousands of lifetimes to see some of the mental tortures awaiting in Mercury."

Perhaps in Mercury lies an explanation of why

some valiant souls elect to be born blind, deaf, or tragically crippled. If they visited Mercury between earth lives and discovered that they had inflicted similar damages on others, they may have summoned the courage to wipe their slate clean by assuming that burden themselves in this particular incarnation.

The Guides had little to say of Pluto, writing only, "A minor stop. It simply suggests ways of improving one's determination to succeed where all has failed in some lives. A reevaluation station, we assume, as we have not yet visited Pluto."

Then they said of Saturn, "The halo, ah, yes. Saturn is where one goes for spiritual uplift, and it is reserved by most until the other planetary influences have been met, for to achieve perfection Saturn is so important that we are unable yet to tell much about it. Some who have visited Saturn and returned to this level [where the Guides are] simply say that they were not yet ready for that ultimate testing of the soul and would first run the course of the others. The sun and moon are our magnetic opposites and help to balance our progress here, as they do for physical beings."

These last three planets sounded less alarming than the other five, but perhaps only because the Guides had not yet visited them. Disturbed at the prospect of such a celestial tour in spirit, I plaintively asked if we could avoid such a fate by living spiritual lives while in physical body. Their reply was somewhat enigmatic: "If one achieves near perfection in physical living, these planetary visits are painless, for one walks unchallenged through tests that for another are frighteningly real. 'No sweat,' as the kids say, to take this sweep around the heavens if you are free of guilt."

Ouch! I could find little comfort in that statement, so I asked *why* we have to visit planets between lives, and they responded, "To face self. To compensate for injuries to others and rid self of egotistical attitudes and superiority complexes. They are a leveling process. Again and again we tell you: Face oneself while in physical life. Take stock. Improve, and attempt to undo wrongs of thought or action committed against others, because it is far easier to accomplish it there than to undergo the spiritual tortures of these planetary visits. Why not take the time now to begin this process of cleansing the akashic record? Assess the harm done to others, and straightaway commence to undo it by atonement, or helpfulness to those who are afraid of you. What matter if they have also harmed you? That is not your karma, but theirs, and when they meet self they will be required to atone for it; so leave it to them, but help whenever possible by forgiving and forgetting. It is so easy to do this in physical life, and so strenuous after passing into spirit. Erase the faults while there is yet time, and make the most of that opportunity in the flesh."

Dismally aware that I am not "free of guilt," I was filled with dread at the prospect of undergoing these stringent tests until I realized that most of us have doubtless already experienced some of them.

Death can hold no terrors when we accept the philosophy of reincarnation, because if we have lived many times before we have also experienced many "deaths," and in spirit have probably undergone some of these "states of consciousness" under planetary influences.

Somewhat heartened, I asked the Guides if they would be willing to illustrate these weird planetary visits by recounting some actual experiences of those on the "other side" who had made the journeys in spirit. I was not prepared for what followed! Many years ago Lily told me that "the Group" consisted of twelve souls who were working together to bring me material for the books, but he consistently declined to reveal their separate identities, and only when Arthur Ford eventually joined the team after his demise in 1971 did Art sometimes use the first person singular, since I had personally known him.

In answer to my query, the writing began in the usual fashion, as a group effort. But within a short while it switched to a personal account, and there after each day's description of a planetary visit was apparently written by a different member of the Group, in markedly contrasting style. This is how it commenced:

"Ruth, this is Lily, Art, and the Group. Now as to the visits to other planets, let us say that Venus is one of the most interesting interludes and we will tell you about one of our visits there. It was as if we were wafted on a summer's breeze to another more peaceful clime. Suddenly we were suffused with love for all the world, enveloped in a soft substance so richly clothed that pure happiness seemed at last within reach. We were there without effort, and as we floated above the surface as if on a fleecy cloud, we sensed that within each drop of misty dew there was an entire world of sweetness and tranquility. Never have we had such feeling before or since, for it was unique to earthling man. As we soaked in this atmosphere of peace and harmony, we observed that other souls were equally enjoying the rapture of undiluted love, and we felt such a strong pull that we immediately and effortlessly joined a group that was frolicking on what appeared to be a pink-and-purple cloud. There was no physical sensation, of course, and nothing to touch, but we were as if enfolded within the fleeciest of down comforters, warm and soft and good. There is nothing with which to compare the sensation, at once mellow and soft, and so filled with joy as to be beyond comprehension. After a time it was as if we had slept and then awakened, for the feeling began to cloy."

At this point the writing switched to the first person singular, and when I later read it I knew that Arthur Ford could not have been its author. It was totally unlike anything I have received from him. On subsequent days, as other planetary experiences were related, the style was even more markedly altered from the usual pattern to which I had grown accustomed. And now to continue with the visitation of Venus:

"I became uncomfortable, almost as one does when eating too much cotton candy at a fair. Would not such ever-loving love wear thin after a time? I almost hoped for a harsh word to be uttered, or for a frown to cloud a brow, but no! All was serenity and sweetness and never-ending love. Why was I so uncomfortable with such harmony of spirit? Was it because I myself was out of tune with the Universe? Why was I not ready yet for pure and caring love? What had I left undone that ill-fitted me for this serenity? I searched my memory for deeds done in anger, words spoken for which I had not yet apologized, flashes of anger that had left me sharp as needles. What should I do in accountability, for this became an unbearable prison of the soul! Here I was in a heaven of divine accord, feeling out of sorts and unable to adapt myself to its atmosphere. Should I stick it out, feeling myself immersed in a ball of cotton candy, or return to earth to make a new try at harmony with my fellowmen?

"Approaching was a soul whom I spontaneously recalled as an elderly man I had known in Brooklyn. His beard then was white and long, but now it seemed diaphanous and sparkling. 'Son, son,' he greeted me, 'again we meet, in this heavenly sphere. What may I do to assist you?' With a spark of remembrance I cried out, 'But I wronged you in Brooklyn, sir. Remember the store on the corner where you had sweetmeats and trinkets for children? As we passed along to school I stole a ball, and I felt that you were stupid not to have caught me, so another time I took a peppermint when you were waiting on another child. I had no respect for you, and now I am ashamed.'

" 'Forget it,' the old man said gently, embracing me in the warmth of his love. 'It is so little, and you were so young that I turned away my eyes to keep from hurting you. It was wrong of me, for I thus encouraged you to steal again. Forgive me, my boy.' That was one of the finest moments I have ever known. Such love flowed out from me that the man became a part of my very self. We were as one, such melding as no physical being has ever known. I began to love Venus so deeply that I felt reluctant to leave, but something within cautioned that there were other ways to advance without becoming too deeply immersed in the purity of selfless love. Yet as other planets were visited, I felt drawn again and again to Venus, where I shall one day return. This is all for now."

The writing stopped, and the next morning it commenced in vastly different manner, declaring, "For a visit to Mars we will let one of the twelve Guides tell you of his experience there." The pressure changed on the typing keys, and to my continuing astonishment I was introduced to a totally different type of Guide, who wrote as follows:

"Ruth, this is one of the twelve. What is it like to visit Mars between lives? Well, what is war like at the height of an artillery battle, with bombs cascading and jet streaking in for the kill? It was by no means my favorite experience, believe me. I had been postponing that trip from one lifetime to another, hoping eventually to acquire such fine attributes that it would leave me unruffled, but such was not to be the case. I had often been a soldier in earth lives, not particularly through preference, but because I was always being called to battle for some so-called noble cause like democracy or defense! Anyway, it sounded like the worst of the battles when I eased onto Mars, determined to face that visitation rather than having it hanging over me eternally from one spirit stay to the next. Talk about surprised! Instead of Martian music I beheld souls singing in unison 'Auld Lang Syne'-type songs as if this were a reunion of pals at an Old Grad's day celebration. What was the idea? I wondered; but soon it became apparent that these souls had tried again and again to complete a stay on Mars and get it behind them, just as I was now doing, but each time they encountered old friends who had also given it up for a time and then decided to return after another lifetime or two or three, so it was Reunion Day all right. They took me in as a buddy, although it was my first trip there, and some even gave me good advice, saying to keep out of direct range of the lightning and thunder of cannon, and tend to my own knitting. This sounded pretty silly to a recent earthling who was trying to feel his way along in a new atmosphere, until I heard that clashing and crashing mentioned earlier, and it was for all the world like Alamein and Dunkirk. As you see, I've had a recent turn in flesh and was in those battles. Anyway, the advice to steer clear of the action on Mars came in good stead, for instead of rushing along to investigate the cause, I decided to meditate as I had been taught on this side of the open door; and as I meditated peace came, the hullabaloo died down, and before I knew it all was quiet and serene. That's the way to cope with Mars. Play it cool, and turn away from turmoil, strife, and the belting of spirit forces. I will need to go there again to wear off all my warlike karma from so many lives as a soldier, but actually I'm dreading Mars less than some of the others, such as sweet ol' Venus. Maybe I was just lucky this time, but Lily seems to think I handled the situation right and will have no need to fear it."

I have no idea who that engaging soldier might have been in any of his earth lives, but certainly he was a different personality from the one who took over the typewriter in the next day's session, writing, "Neptune is one of the most interesting experiences, and one of us has been there, so let him tell the story." That was, of course, Lily or a group effort, and the writing now began:

"In this ethereal atmosphere [Neptune] one may lay down his burdens to feel totally devoid of cares. For a time it is a blissful sensation and one in which there is no undue pressure to recount one's omissions and commissions. For a while it seems that time stands still, not in the earthly sense but in the progress of a soul. I visited Neptune the first time after only seven or eight earth lives, and had decided while there that the journey was complete and no further incarnations would be necessary. No sin existed anywhere, as far as I could see. My akashic record was unblemished. A feeling of apathy ensued during which I thought, So this is it. Now where do I go from here? Actually there was no need of pushing on in any direction, for it was comfortable there and I was at peace with myself. Then, after some time I realized that this was simply a waiting stage, and if I tarried too long there would be nothing of anything—a vacuum, so to speak. Thus I returned to the area where we are now and consulted others about the likelihood of pressing onward to reunion with God. They stared at me as if I were suddenly bereft of my senses, asking what encouraged me to think that I was fit and ready for the supreme reunion. I explained about Neptune, and one who had been there twitted, 'Wait until you've gone there a few dozen more times after earthly ventures and you will become as accustomed as I am to that false sense of security. It is a resting state, and also a testing ground, for until one undergoes that feeling of nothingness he does not completely grasp the sense of somethingness which drives one again and again to try another earth life in order to erase the wrongs and gild the lily of endeavors. I know how treacherous that sense of well-being can be, for to test myself I have returned several times to Neptune, and each time that sense of "well done" envelops me in its seductive garments. It is how we will perhaps feel when we at last do earn the right to the feeling, but then there will not be the nothingness along with it, for the goal is so rich that we will indeed then be fulfilled.' So I guess I'll be seeing more of Neptune at another time."

To my enormous surprise, it was Lily rather than Arthur Ford, my ordinarily garrulous friend, who recounted Arthur's unhappy experience on Uranūs, about which he has seemed so reluctant to speak. In order to understand this particular episode, it is necessary to explain to those who have not read *Companions along the Way* that in that book Lily identified himself as Savonarola, the fifteenth-century martyred priest of Florence, and said Arthur Ford was then his friend, also a Dominican monk. And now to this day's writing:

"As to Uranus, where Arthur felt so uncomfortable, it will be difficult to bring you the account of his experience, since he feels unable to talk about it to any extent. It was the time of his respite here after the life as a monk in Florence. Full of savage resentment against the Catholic Church and its treatment of Savonarola and others who were martyred in the name of religion, he set about to complete his rounds of the planets and turn his back on the physical earth. He therefore went with great rage to Uranus, hoping to get it over with, and on to eventual reunion without return to physical being, and it was scarcely the right atmosphere for his own mood and torment. He swept into the plane of Escandon [*sic*] almost as if it were a waiting railroad station and he had more important things on his mind than idle gossip with other waiting passengers. He plunged headlong into the influences, and before he knew it was so entangled in a web of his own weaving that he felt stifled and desperate for release. Literally he was entwined with cords of his own weaving and strings of his own webbing, so that he was totally entrapped—a smothering feeling of hopelessness and frustration. While he simmered in his rage, he was ever tightening the bonds that held him, so that finally he was ready to lose all, sacrifice all that he had gained in that good life as a monk if only he would lose the fetters. At this juncture pressure relaxed, and with a great wellspring of gratitude to whatever force had released him, he speedily returned here, more than willing to leave the test of Uranus to some other period here between earthly lives. It will not affect everyone as it did Arthur, but it is well to leave behind the rages and resentments, for to bring them with you from earth lives to other planetary atmosphere is hazardous in the extreme."

Good old Arthur! Perhaps he was beginning to make his peace with organized religion, because in his most recent incarnation he was an ordained minister of the Christian (Disciples of Christ) Church, and although he left the pulpit to devote his remarkable talents to the psychic field, becoming America's most famous medium, he nevertheless helped found an organization to investigate the subject of psychic phenomena within the churches, where it belongs. But he has not yet tried Uranus again!

The next morning, still another surprise awaited me. Never once had Lily hinted that a woman was one of my twelve Guides, and since he often stressed that sexual differences do not exist in spirit, it had not occurred to me to inquire. I had to await the explanation until the end of the session, which began as a group effort: "On Jupiter we have found many occasions when we longed to return to earth life, for it is a pressing or oppressive atmosphere in many respects. To be on Jupiter is to be rather much of a king without a throne, for when we would wish to serve ourselves, it is impossible to do so, nor are we there to help those we love who are still in flesh. We feel cut off from the universe, as if in a glass case where we are able to perceive but not to act. Frustration, yes, and somewhat of a vacuum. One of us was there recently and we will let her tell you about it."

Her! I am only vaguely aware of what is coming through my fingers on the typewriter, when in the alpha or meditative state, but that unexpected feminine pronoun jolted my subconsciousness. This is what "she" wrote:

"Ruth, we are all appreciative of your efforts to express what we are attempting to tell about this remarkable experience through which all of us are passing. The earth turns, and the orbiting is in perfect pattern, yet we are powerless to see to the end of the age. In Jupiter where I elected to go, at least in a state of consciousness after crossing over here not too many earth years ago, I felt the need for review of past endeavors and a look at the direction of my soul's progress. In Jupiter I felt this to be of extreme importance, for until we view ourselves as an entirety, without relationships with others, we are unable to mark our progression. In Jupiter were others like myself who wished to analyze their passage and review their ideals. Some were upset and others somewhat mollified by what they could discern of their karmic pattern. For myself it was a rather exhilarating experience, for until then I had been seeing all the faults and entangling alliances that had kept me from soaring ahead. There in Jupiter I perceived that some of the sins which weighed heavily on my being were so minor as to be ignored. Such things as stealing an apple or disagreeing with another's analysis of a given problem were unimportant compared with some of the unfinished business: opportunities for aiding others which I had failed to take advantage of, times when someone needed reassurance but I was too busy or impatient to heed that person's need, times when I would gladly have rendered assistance if I had been sensitive enough to perceive it. Forgive us our trespasses, but also forgive us those undone deeds for which the door stood open. In Jupiter one sees the necessity for taking time; not squandering time in idle pursuits, but taking time to see the interlocking relationships with others, so that we are acutely aware of their needs. Jupiter is rather a pleasant experience if one will become introspective and assess his shortcomings, for to search one's own soul is surely more fascinating than to search a mountain in quest of a path to its summit. However, we will need to remember that until we find the true path that leads to reunion with the Creator we will ever be stumbling along, sliding back, slithering sideways, and seemingly lost. Hold fast to the ideals formed before you entered flesh, and seek for that which is sublime."

Whoever this mysterious woman was, I liked her,

and after she said good-bye, the writing continued: "This is Lily, Art and the Group. Yes, one of your guides is a woman, and a perceptive soul at that. But let us stress that all of us have been of both sexes, and that she simply trails the ascendant female characteristics from her most recent life in the flesh."

The following day, after the usual group introduction, my Guide wrote, "Today we will let another member of the group tell of his experience in Mercury." An individual soul then took over the typing: "Ah, Mercury, the mercurial! How it sparkles and slithers and shines! I went there of my own free will, determined to lay at rest the notion that one who has sinned in wordly guise would be unable to complete a Mercurian visit in one straight try. I had learned from others of its unstable condition, the atmosphere at once slimy and shiny, but I was unafraid. For one who has lived as many earth lives as I have, no planet could prove disconcerting, or so I thought. In the instant that my decision was made, I found myself in the murky atmosphere of this planet, about which so little seems to be understood. There I was, and I was not alone. Others, with strange energy surrounding them, were moving about as if in a vortex of circular motion, somewhat as if they were in the bowl of an electric washing machine run in slow motion. How strange, I thought, that they do not step off dead center and proceed about their quest for perfection. I was having no difficulty maintaining my position, or so I thought, until I looked about and found that everything seemed to be revolving except myself. Ah, so I too was in a vortex! Well, it was not too unpleasant, so for a time I relaxed and gave myself over to the sensation of slowly being whirled about. Remembering the feeling one gets on a train when it seems to be in motion, but is actually standing still because other trains in a depot are moving, I smiled to think how often earthly sensations are paralleled in the spirit realm. After a time I felt I should make some effort to proceed with the business at hand, so I looked about for a way to remove myself from the spinning. At that moment I was freed, and when the others saw what occurred, they too wished themselves quiet, and thereby ceased to revolve. Now we were togther, and as we wondered what to do next, a shining woman-figure appeared before us saying, 'So that you do not waste precious time, follow me.' We at once gathered around and she whisked off into space, with the rest of us in tow. Where to now? I wondered, but ere long she deposited us beside a shimmering fountain and advised us to drink of the sparkling fluid that emanated from it. Since we had no physical bodies we simply slaked our imaginary thirst, and almost at once felt ourselves chained to a side of the shaft on which stood the bubbling fountain. We were powerless to leave, for our unseen bonds held us as securely as ever a dog is chained to his kennel. Why? we wondered. Why, indeed? We had become a slave to physical desires: the woman, the water, the needs we had left behind in physical being. So there we were, rooted in a manner of speaking, until at the sound of a tinkling bell the fountain vanished and we were in a silvery glade. Now there appeared a table laden with delicacies of every sort, those foods we had most relished in our recent incarnation. Some moved forward, eagerly snatching at the delicacies, but I had enough perception to understand that this, like the sparkling fluid, was a trap. No longer did we need nourishment of the body, or water, or sex; so I floated freely away, and in time came to the river of life. It flowed softly without murmur, almost as a drop of mercury slithers along a slanting counter. I understood now that all fleshly desires ended with spirit, and since this included stress about those left behind whom we had cherished, as well as any interest in former professional duties, I understood that this was a healing step, ridding self of longing for earthly pursuits and business left undone. No need to fear for the safety of those we had left behind. They would one day also make this journey and would then understand why I no longer hung about the house in spirit form, to try to solve their problems and help with the checkbook balancing. I was now ready to go on, and this I have done. Mercury is a spiritual experience, and if this is the worst that the planetary visitations require, I have conquered my dread of them."

This seemed an obvious reference to those souls who, having passed out of the physical body into spirit, continue to hang around the house or office and feel frustrated because no one pays attention to them. In *A World Beyond* Arthur Ford gave several examples of disquieted spirits who refused to recognize that they were "dead," and tried to carry on as if they were still running the show in the old neighborhood. The Guides have often warned against the pitfall of nursing grief for the passing of a loved one, pointing out that this keeps that soul earthbound and unable to proceed with his own spiritual growth.

The particular Guide who gave a report of his visit to Mercury seemed to realize while there that it was no longer necessary for him to help his widow balance the checkbook and manage her financial affairs. By doing so, he was cheating her of the opportunity to develop latent talents while still in fleshly body, and he was slowing his own progression as well.

When I asked the Guides about the two remaining major planets in our galaxy, they replied, "As we have said, we have not yet visited Saturn or Pluto, although some others are here who tell us about them." The typing changed, and this is what came through: "When I went to Saturn it was as if spirituality had occupied that area for all the days of its years. A blissful atmosphere, so full of adoration for God that I felt sublimely motivated to spend my total period there in adoration of the Creator. That halo which is seen by earthling astronomers surely emanates from the adoration welling up from all those souls there who seem to think of nothing less than total adoration. Forgive me. I repeat the word, but what other synonym so completely expresses the meaning of adoration?"

Lily then returned to introduce a different soul, who wrote of Pluto: "An easy rest stop for those who are truly on the quest for reunion with God. Some may feel strangled by the peace and security, since no adverse reactions are permissible there. Sometimes it is difficult to fix one's attention on the goal, because of the imps who play about as if illustrating an old text of Dante's *Inferno*, but they are harmless, as far as I could observe, and are solely intent on amusing themselves. Where they come from, or what their purpose is I cannot say, but since I was there so briefly I am no expert on Pluto. I have heard dark rumors of rather frightening experiences there, but since I have not received this directly from one who has experienced it, I cannot say whether it is true. The tricky thing about Pluto is that if you so much as think of another goal than reunion while there, suddenly there is no longer a Pluto for you. In other words, it is of necessity a brief stay until, I presume, you have passed all other hurdles and are ready for reunion, because it is like quicksilver. The moment any thought but reunion occurs, Pluto vanishes. More accurately, I suppose, you vanish from Pluto. This is all I can tell you about it."

Musing about all this planetary material at a later date, I wondered if perhaps it may help us earthlings to know about it while still in physical body, so that we can prepare for each visitation ahead of time and choose wisely which to visit in proper order. Visits in spirit naturally reminded me of our scientific explorations in space, and I asked the Guides to comment on the voyages of our sophisticated American and Russian spaceships to other planets, as well as the prospect for manned space flights there. In philosophical vein, they replied:

"When the soul of man develops to the high state it once enjoyed, earth life will be drastically altered, for then there will be no need for interplanetary travel. The souls will be able to project to those outer reaches and be aware of all we need to know about development on other planets. Thus the fantastically costly projects will serve no real purpose, for the various planets are self-contained units and each will develop according to the Divine plan, finding harmony with the Creator and all of his creations. Earth souls are by no means as highly advanced as some of the spirits inhabiting other planets, and thus will have to find the impetus to develop spiritually to a much higher degree before they are ready to inhabit other planets; for until the atmospheric conditions of each planet, with its protective ring, are harmonized, they are not privileged to spread the earth influence to those other spheres. When that does occur, earth souls will be able to intermingle through thought projection with those of the others, but none is similar in development. Some planets are without atmosphere, so a different type of vessel [body] is required to sustain life there: a being which need have no bellows or breathing apparatus, because there is nothing to breathe. But the power or force we worship as God is not restricted to conditions we know on earth, and is able out of nothingness to create that which is good. Thus the moon has nothing that is lifelike in our sense, yet there are forces there which to our Creator are as real as are we of the flesh. Other planets have their idiosyncrasies and support various forms that are occupied or used by spirit entities.

"Let us give you an example. At one time, in the beginning of man's development, there were enormous mammals who walked on the surface of the earth and spread fear into the hearts of all those of lesser size. Yet the dinosaurs and mammoths have vanished, while puny man continues to spread his prowess throughout the world. Thus it is not size or build or shape that determines importance, but the mastering of those talents God bestowed on his creations, whether on this planet or the myriads of other heavenly bodies. When we visit them in this state of consciousness where we are now, they are as habitable as the earth; yet we would not have been able to exist there in physical bodies that are equipped only to cope with the earth of which we were a part. Thus the lesson to be learned is that everything has its rightful place in the universe, and the conditions are just right for each developing spirit. Each soul born into physical being is unique in that it is equipped with the tools not only for survival but also for advancement within its own sphere of operation, and *there* is where man will grow and develop, or retrogress. When you understand this simple law, you realize how urgent it is for each soul to make the most of his own environment, which he helped to choose and which for him is the best of all worlds, whether it be ghetto or palace; for the equipment he brought back into physical body suits him best for that role, and as he advances spiritually he will develop beyond his ghetto or palace, casting off the restrictions each imposes and fitting him for the role of sainthood, if he employs his God-given talents."

The Guides then concluded their sermonette by declaring: "We are endowed with the faculties necessary to sustain us in earthly form, and what we are able to accomplish in a life-span regulates how rapidly we shall advance in our quest for the Godhead. Until we rejoin that vortex of power, we will ever wander in lonely splendor, homesick, ever seeking for the lost glory that was ours when we too were a part of the Godhead. Each of us is a part of God, and God is thus a part of each of us. Together we comprise the whole, so let us remember to help all with whom we are in contact, speaking and thinking well of them. They are a part of us, and together we make up a small part of God, for God is also the rills and rocks, the flora and fauna, the fish and fowl, and all that we hear and see and know."

That did it for me! I resolved then and there to make up for lost time and begin living a perfect life. Alas! A few hours later I was sassing my husband, as usual.

and consumed with love. Some does this not spirit

it takes joyfully for the essence; and not for the

14

Prognostications

For the past several years the Guides have been painstaking in their efforts to help me understand the true meaning of time and prophecy. Just as we explain to a child in pictorial language something he is seeking to grasp, so the Guides have sought through simplified terms to make me comprehend why they are able to see into the future and I am not.

One day they wrote, "The area of time is an interesting one, for although we are aware of it here in the earthly sense, we recognize its lack of reality. In a canoe you see as far ahead as a bend in the river, yet the river continues and is as real beyond as the segment where you are rowing. When you round the curve you observe a new vista, but only memory recalls the stream through which you have just passed. Here we see the wider spectrum as from an airplane flying overhead, and even the inevitability that the canoe will topple over a waterfall that awaits just around the bend. Think on this as you contemplate time, for in astral body we are situated to see that which lies ahead as well as behind; yet even here we see no further than one of our own lifetimes ahead. All reality is within self, and if we saw to the end of the road we would know at what moment we would eventually rejoin our Creator after X number of incarnations, but this is not possible here. That is within the province of God, who sees as far beyond us as is possible to conceive. Trust then in self to ply the quiet stream unafraid, for the future is already as definite for earthly souls as is the past.

"Space is another nonreality, and whatever occurs reflects only on us. We are the center of our individual universes, and within us is the Godpart which regulates our particular atom, our universe. When we are able to conceive of ourselves as a sphere, smooth on all sides with no entangling karma, we will have achieved wholeness and be ready for reunion. In meditation, therefore, visualize self as a perfect whole, eliminating trailing traces of karmic ties which bind us too closely to the earth, for we would instead be a part of the divine Being."

Some of this sounded as if we are without free will, but another time the Guides elaborated: "Now that we are ready for predictions, let us say that the difference between prediction and prophecy is that the first is what we see happening due to seemingly irreversible trends. Prophecy in the Biblical sense is a prognostication of that which will occur unless man mends his ways, and is therefore likely to occur. Say that a river flows around a bend and we [the Guides] see beyond the bend to a disaster in midstream where two ships will collide. This is certain to occur because of their rates of speed and lack of attention to navigation. Yet if someone could meanwhile throw up a dam which altered the course of the river, the ships would be unable to collide. Thus there is a possibility of such a dam being erected, but little likelihood, and unless it is, collision is inevitable. But as to seeing ahead, some of it is as definite as that which has already occurred, for we see a longer eye of the needle."

Persisting in their efforts to clarify the point they wanted to make, they gave still another illustration, writing, "We who are on this side of the open door are able to project ahead and behind in what you call time, not to the last days but to a rather long passage of earth years. Thus we are able to see into past lives, reading akashic records that are the imprint made by every single deed and action, and are able to look further ahead to future events. Let us pause for a moment to see what this means in terms of a human being in one earth life. He sees only what is transpiring at a given moment and delves into the past of that particular incarnation through memory alone, but here we actually see those events as they unfolded perhaps thousands of years ago by earth time. Thus the sensation of being at one with self in many previous earth lives is as real to us in each of those lives as in the last one. Souls on earth are also able to glimpse this when their minds are put to rest and projected backward through hypnosis or dreams, but the sensation is far more vivid on our side. The same means is available to us for seeing into future events, and here too we see them unfold much as we watched the unfoldment of events in ages past. Those on this side, for instance, saw Jack Kennedy's death in an open car well before it occurred, and that is why so many souls living where you are were able to glimpse the danger, because they were picking up the excitement and projection of danger from this side."

This latter statement apparently referred to the fact that a number of psychics predicted President Kennedy's assassination shortly before it occurred. Arthur Ford was living in Philadelphia at that time, and I shall never forget that while attending one of his trance sessions in 1962 I heard his "spirit control," Fletcher, warn that President Kennedy would be "killed in a moving conveyance while away from Washington." This was a year before the assassination, but Fletcher and other spirits apparently saw it unfolding in advance. Taking into account what the Guides wrote in their analogy of the "bend in the river" and the "dam," I would assume that the tragedy could have been averted if JFK had heeded warnings not to go to Dallas, or if the parade route had suddenly been altered, but the spirit realm saw little likelihood of such a change.

This same Fletcher, during another Ford trance session on October 28, 1964, declared that Barry Goldwater's Presidential electoral vote would be "a minimum of forty-three and a maximum of fifty-two." When the votes of the electoral college were counted after the November election, Barry received exactly fifty-two.

Before writing this section of the book, I reviewed the predictions that Arthur Ford had made from the spirit plane for *A World Beyond*, after his death in January 1971. To date his batting average is an amazing one hundred percent. Some of his predictions still pertain to future events, but of those which have transpired in the five years since I wrote the chapter, all are correct. For instance:

1. In the spring of 1971 the "spirit" Ford flatly declared that President Nixon would be "a shoo-in" for reelection in November 1972, with Spiro Agnew again on the tickct. At that time Nixon was at his lowest ebb in public opinion polls, and many commentators were predicting that Agnew would be dropped as his running mate.

2. Ford said neither Senator Ted Kennedy nor Senator Henry Jackson would get the Democratic nomination in 1972.

3. He declared that Ethel Kennedy would not remarry "for some time," and that there would be

no divorce for Jacqueline Kennedy Onassis and her husband, Aristotle Onassis.

4. Although war was then raging in Vietnam, Ford saw it shortly drawing to a close, and warned that the men who made up our fighting forces there would come home to a period of severe unemployment. Asserting that they would be less interested in returning to college than the veterans of World War II and the Korean conflict, he added, "These are activists, and they want to plunge right into careers or work."

5. At the time Ford was conveying this information in 1971, a Communist President was firmly in the saddle in Chile, but Arthur Ford wrote, "Chile? An overthrow there before too long, and Communists no longer in power."

6. He also said Germany "will slip a bit financially these next few years, but will continue to be a power, with the two sectors somewhat closer together" but not merged.

All of these events have come to pass since 1971.

On the morning of November 27, 1973, the Guides abruptly wrote: "Nixon will not finish out his term." They said "a health problem" would contribute to his decision to resign, and thereafter Watergate would cease to be "a prime subject, although it will not be forgotten ever, and will stand as a beacon of warning for future American Presidents."

Intrigued by their flat assertion, I had my husband sign the date and his name to the prediction, and I also read it to my weekly study group in

Cuernavaca, Mexico, where we then lived. Nearly nine months later, in August 1974, Richard M. Nixon resigned as President of the United States and almost immediately thereafter went into the hospital, where he nearly lost his life.

Because of their remarkable record for accuracy, I asked the Guides for further predictions to include in this book, and although they themselves state that human beings have the power to alter seemingly irreversible trends, they diligently brought answers to my list of questions. In the remainder of this chapter I will not use quotation marks, because all the material is in the words of the Guides. But since at times my unseen friends have a tendency to editorialize, perhaps I should follow the lead of television networks and issue a disclaimer: The opinions expressed herein are not necessarily those of this station.

New forms of energy will be produced by solar disks that slowly rotate in wide arcs while generating steam for power. These will be located near large industrial areas, and transformers will take over the task of propelling machines and harnessing energy even for automobiles. A way of storing solar energy, as in ancient Atlantis, will revolutionize the power industry. It is necessary to find other forms than fossil fuels, for these are being exhausted at such a rapid rate that it is hastening the shift of the earth's axis in the late 1990s. Soon there will be a breakthrough in solar energy that will require great marketing skill, since at first it will seem too expensive, but when produced in great volumes it will become one of the cheapest fuels ever devised.

Medicine will make enormous strides in the next two decades, including a definite understanding of cancer, its causes and cures. Wild cells go astray through wrong thinking and emotional upheavals in one's life. Few are without the potential for cancer, which is set off through diseases of a psychosomatic nature—that is to say, of emotional origin. In this Aquarian Age, when minds become opened to the infinite, so much will be revealed as to make earlier strides seem puny indeed. Meditation unlocks the door, and those who learn properly to give themselves surcease and relief from turmoil through this quieting of the mind and spirit will progress rapidly. Communion with God through prayer is the ultimate, and the way will be opened when one makes true effort to speak with him who was and is our eternal companion. We see medicine taking new leaps within the new few years, through discovery of a life-making substance. When implanted into an area from which malignant cells have been removed, it will take over and produce healthy growth as if it had been there from the beginning. There will be some inherent dangers, if improperly used, but a breakthrough is indeed at hand in the treatment of cancer. A new vaccine will radically reduce the perils of influenza, particularly in the elderly.

Tobacco smoking will soon become passé as substitutes are introduced which minimize withdrawal pains, and this will be a blessing, since nearly everyone wishes to stop destroying his body with tar and nicotine, but has found no easy substitute for the pleasure of smoking. This new discovery will give the same satisfaction, while replacing the dangerous and noxious qualities of cigarettes with healthful ones. Actually it is a return to nature, rather than another chemical invention.

As to drug usage, this is a menace of real proportions, because it damages in the physical and the spirit state as well, since some souls cling to the desire here. We see it gradually lessening, but not disappearing entirely until after the shift of the axis. Such a pity, for young people are destroying the sharp edge of their minds and stunting their spiritual development when they use drugs.

Atlantis has already begun to rise near Bimini, and more of it will emerge during the next three decades. After the shift, large parts of it will surface, as well as some small areas of Lemuria, while some other remnants of that latter landmass will disappear.

No woman will serve as President of the United States in the remainder of this century. After the shift of the axis America will be a different sort of land, and it is hard to predict politics for each individual area of the world thereafter. Teddy Kennedy will never be President.

The feminist movement will continue to gain strength as the stridency goes out of the voices of those who lead the movement, and like a snowball picking up speed it will become a recognized right for all humans to be coequal and develop in their own way. Since some men prefer to work in the home at so-called womanly tasks without losing their masculinity, and some women to work outside the home without losing femininity, this will occur much oftener, until it is recognized as normal. Numerous marriages will reverse the pattern of recent civilizations. Many women will be the breadwinners while husbands do the housekeeping and babytending, without any onus attached. Marriage as an institution will continue despite today's loose living, for the homing instinct is strong in homo sapiens and man is by nature monogamous. This is not to say that sexual experimentation is out, for in all ages men and women have occasionally lusted after another and sometimes found greater happiness in the presence of a different person than the one to whom they are wedded. Yet the sacrament of marriage will survive, as it should, because it is important to children, who depend on both male and female home influence to guide them into properly balanced lives.

The ability to reproduce human life outside a mother's womb is not in the foreseeable future. Were it to become feasible, what sort of soul would wish to enter such an artificially created body? Only an evil or robot type who would be a menace to world society. With all the genius at work in the scientific-medical field, surely there are avenues which offer greater helpfulness than this pursuit of the ability to play god with human souls. As to freezing a body and returning it to life in a later generation, what nonsense! The soul leaves at death, so what is there left but a worn-out mechanism, like an unoccupied farmhouse that has been abandoned? Why are some humans so intent on pursuing wrong goals in their honorable search for betterment of human life-style?

The stock market will continue on the general rise for some time now, with very little backward slippage. The financial news is brighter, and through the remainder of this decade business prospects look rather rosy.

The educational situation in America will worsen as long as the government compels parents to send their children to assigned schools, rather than giving some choice and versatility. The forced busing system is wrong. The troublemakers should be segregated from the willing learners, so that the latter are not left educationally and emotionally crippled by young thugs who seek trouble rather than learning. A disastrous situation is shaping up unless communities are given more leeway to regulate their own school systems.

Zionism will continue to be a force in persuading those of Jewish faith to return to the Palestinian homeland, but the numbers of those leaving Israel after trying the experiment will outnumber the new recruits. This is just as well. Why overpopulate a land that needs hardy workers, who love every inch of the soil, with swashbucklers who seek only adventure, or revenge on the Arabs?

Hunger will continue as a problem in underdeveloped nations that are more intent on power, prestige, and guns than on the well-being of their citizens. If only an American President had the moral courage to say, "Hereafter we will export know-how for raising crops and making implements for peaceful living, but not one gun stock or armament to any nation except for domestic peace-keeping!" This would create a spurt of unwelcome activity by the Soviets, true, but their food shortages are so acute that they would soon welcome the opportunity to concentrate their energies on the home front. Why will Americans not learn that they are unable to support the world, or even that portion of it which pretends friendship? Atlanteans never learned it, either, and were always meddling in others' affairs.

A long gap is developing in the space race with Russia, and after a time America will be recognized as second-rate in space programs. She will be unable to keep up with Russia because of a U.S. government fearful of spending money which the liberals demand must go to public welfare. This will lead to fighting factions—those who feel that welfare is taking over the nation, as labor unions are already doing, and those who feel that prestige abroad is necessary to discourage warlike moves and preserve peace. It will be a raging controversy of the coming decade and will not be settled until war breaks out in the late 1980s. The welfare programs will have produced little to aid in that dire period, and the lack of modern equipment for fighting will be sorely felt. The destiny of America lies in preserving peace, not feeding able-bodied people who have no will to seek out the hard life when the soft hand of welfare is so readily available. The strong America of the past decades is on the wane. Softness is replacing strength, and there will be few efforts to stop the trend as liberal Democrats take over the government. The coming three years will be a crucial point in history. There are forces at work that will turn America into a socialistic state and wreck the economy for decades to come. We see this trend toward electing so-called liberal politicians, despite the will of thinking people to become more conservative. Better by far to install in the White House a man with fiscal integrity, who will bounce the loafers and chiselers from welfare rolls, but there is little prospect of a return to sound fiscal practice. Increased defict spending and huge welfare rolls are in store.

England will become more conservative as the United States grows more radical, but it has a sad row to hoe. That nation of wonderful people is becoming so strained by socialistic controls and welfare programs that the great heart of the nation, the middle class, has nothing left to encourage the kind of diligent work that helped make it the foremost nation of the world for so long. England will weather its current financial disaster and begin emerging as a strong factor in world financial circles, with a Tory prime minister who is a woman. She will set a fine example for prudence and fiscal responsibility, but will have difficulty in reversing a tide of such tumultuous sweep as that which the

Labour party has brought to Britain since World War II.

France will turn farther to the left, and will endanger the balance of power in Europe by its wooing of Soviet strength. It will fall into fiscal irresponsibility, but will find that its policies of baiting the United States and Britain will rebound to its misfortunate.

In Sweden the king will emerge as a strong example of prudence, and set a moral tone for that area of the world.

Look for a surprising development in Germany, where a new and untried leader will emerge and restore confidence in the future of the Germanic people. Some will find him too far to the left, but he will open a bridge for East and West Germans through a loose confederation that will lead to some betterment of conditions there.

Russia in three years will have new leaders who will declare for detente with the Western world, loosen the iron grip on its satellites, and hold out an olive branch to China. These leaders will willingly negotiate some strategic power plays with the United States, in the hope of keeping China off their doorstep, but they are to be watched, as they are nationalists who will be secretly upgrading Russian warheads and missiles.

In Egypt a new president will take over in about two years, and will run that country efficiently and well.

Israel will stop its belligerence and learn to live

in something akin to peace with its Arab neighbors through the end of this decade and into the eighties.

Iran will open its doors to large expeditions of archaeologists, who will make some remarkable finds that will set the ancient times of which we write in proper perspective.

Poland will soon break with Russia over the matter of refugees and the intemperate outbursts against those who wish to visit the West. Although religion is still stifled there, it will soon receive more encouragement from Polish leaders who recognize the need of citizens to worship in religious freedom.

India is in for rocky seas. Time for a spiritual rebirth there, and a new leader with ethical standards who will lead but not force, and will insist on some belt tightening instead of leaping too rapidly into the industrial age.

China is not yet ready for the freeing of mind controls, and will have to await the group of young now being born there, who will eventually seize control by force rather than through elective process.

Argentina is in dire straits and will have an internal revolution within the next few years.

Mexico will see a swing toward the center and will progress economically after Jose Lopez Portillo becomes president. Watch for the current president, Luis Echeverria, to stir up trouble after he is out of office.

As to the state of the world ten years hence, it will be on the brink of war, with some of our present friends lining up with the Communists against us. England will have turned back to Socialism by then, France will be wavering, and Germany so socialistically inclined that they will have little support for our position. Some who are now less than friendly will be on our side. Italy and the Scandinavian countries, Switzerland and the Austria-Hungary of yore, Spain and Portugal will all be leaning toward us. A whole new array of alignments. This is not easily avoided, as it is being set off by factors already in the past, but the citizenry does have the opportunity to set a new course if it acts in time. Let America take heed in the next two Presidential elections (1976 and 1980) and beware of a course that gives too much power to Third World nations seeking to dominate the United Nations. Watch out for a U.S. President who would take away our spiritual foundation by leaning too heavily toward Russian detente, which is a smoke screen for greater Soviet efforts to take over the free world.

Africa will divide into regional areas and merge some of the separate squabbling states that are little more than counties. So silly for each tribal unit to demand a separate vote in the United Nations!

When a strong man shortly emerges as the new director of the United Nations, he will propose that voting procedures be altered to permit a fairer balancing of vote by area, rather than by individual nations. He will not be from the Third World. The United Nations will eventually move from New York City to a more neutral area, which will somewhat ease that city's burdens and permit improved business conditions, for without the task of protecting foreign officialdom, police problems will diminish and crime will take a downturn.

In Abyssinia is a man who will be heard from in the years to come, a man of mixed lineage who was influenced in his youth by a Stalinist devil. This Abyssinian is determined to seize control of that mountain fastness, and from there to wreak havoc on the surrounding area, take over oil and mineral resources, and wage war on the world. His purpose is to seek world domination through anarchy and strife. He is a real menace, and should be apprehended before inestimable damage is done. This devious plot will otherwise take place within the next twelve years and could trigger World War III, for the man is a dangerous fanatic. We see his plans evolving, and do not want them to come to fruition. The man is in the underground now, and in contact with the Soviets.

Arabs in Tunisia are beginning to rethink their position, and a leader will step forward there in the next decade who will propose a plan of such far-reaching possibility that it will be eagerly seized upon in the United Nations as a solution to the rivalry between Jews, Christians, and Moslems in the Near East. This man is now a lower ranking official of tender years, but will be ready for leadership at the time of which we speak. He will propose a stabilization through allocations and realignments, and if it is accepted war in that sensitive area of the world will be avoided. So much depends on the goodwill or ill nature of man that not all events are indelibly stamped on the skein of time in advance of the event. Just as man was given free will by his Creator, so nations made up of homo sapiens are also free to select the course to be followed. If this man's plan is accepted there will be peace in the eighties, but that is all we are able to foresee of it at this time.

Let us now look at Lebanon, where strife has been so violent and unprincipled. Were that area to lessen tensions, the seventies and eighties would be relatively peaceful, for Lebanon holds a key with which to unlock ferocious hatreds and violence, or to smooth the pathway of mankind. Such a move would be hailed for centuries if the right step is taken, yet so will Lebanon write a black page of history in its present course. Let the Lebanese stop to consider the plague they are unleashing on the world.

Northern Ireland will simmer down before too long, and a move by the Crown will bring harmony there, although of a tenuous sort. It will be given home rule in fact as well as name, and will be loosely tied to the commonwealth in international affairs. This will solve much of the tension there.

As to the war outlook, this is seemingly inevitable as the wheels are already set in motion, and by the latter part of the eighties we will likely see another outburst in the Middle and Far East. Lamentable, but so likely to occur that we suggest all should begin making plans for that terrible event, not by a weaponry race but through machinery to settle the affair as rapidly as possible. It will erupt almost without notice, and food will be one of the major triggers to set off the debacle, for since Russia will not be producing enough to feed its populace it will try to seize granaries of the world. The United States will be lined up against the Communist bloc.

Oil will lessen in importance wtihin a decade, as a new form of energy and radically different machines and autos will require less petroleum, but more electricity harnessed from the new sources.

Food will continue to be a major problem in some areas of the world where hunger stalks, but the flesh of animals and intoxicants are better not consumed. If these were discontinued there would be ample grain and corn to feed all humans. Cattle and hogs use too much food for the amount they return in protein, and eating of animal flesh keeps man earthbound rather than free. Unfortunately food will continue to be produced through the use of pesticides, sprays, and artificial fertilizer, while more and more people will desperately try to find organically grown foods that are unadulterated and natural. As pollution continues, pure water will become more valuable than oil, and will be scarcer by far. Even now those with pure water are singularly blessed, and the condition will worsen as man continues his pollution of field and stream. Some will seek methods of quick purification, and others will find ways of sterilizing drinking water within the home, but this will solve little, and by the time the earth spins on its axis, it will have become a dire problem indeed.

New York City in the years to come will present grave problems, for it is occupied by a conglomerate variety of people who will pull in different directions, and welfare will be its biggest industry. New York should place restrictions on accepting immigrants from other states, since its welfare problem is so overpowering—rather in the manner of city states of Greek and Roman times that decided who could live within the boundaries. To continue receiving countless homeless without means of support is a suicidal path for New York City, which in the years ahead will undergo rioting because of hunger and cold, with insufficient heating fuel. [Author's note: The Guides seem to keep an eye on New York City, because on November 16, 1975, when things looked darkest there, and it was about to default on its bonds, they correctly wrote: "If President Ford steps in at once with Federal assistance, the economy will strengthen and Wall Street will have a boom in the coming year."]

Crime will soon take a downturn in New York and throughout America, not for any particular economic reason, but because the ones who will be growing up in this decade and the eighties are determined to find peaceful coexistence not only with other nations, but with neighbors within the community. These are reincarnations of those who lived during the Hundred Years War. Atlanteans are beginning to retreat from the pressure of entry [into physical bodies], as most of those who sought admission are already there, and few other Atlantean souls are seeking life in the flesh at this time.

Interracial marriages will increase, and there is no reason why this should not be, since the purpose of the original five colors has long since been diffused through rapid travel. Now that humans are able to traverse the globe in a matter of hours or days, and great shifts of population have occurred, there is no reason to preserve one color or pigmentation for one particular climate or geographical area.

Earthquakes will imperil the Pacific coast within the next few years, and the San Andreas Fault will split, permitting the outer section to go into the sea. Some of California will survive, and there will be warnings permitting many to escape with their lives and belongings, if they heed the shiftings and rumblings beneath the surface. Vesuvius will erupt first, with great gushings of lava.

Manhattan and some other sections of the East Coast as far north as Newfoundland will be unaffected until the close of the century, when they will vanish with the shift of the axis, as will Hawaii, Japan, and some other Pacific islands. Florida will also be gravely affected, but Egypt will survive, as will most of the Mediterranean area. Venice, that queen of the Adriatic, will sink from sight, and the Gobi Desert will become fertile and pleasant again.

And now to that shift of the axis! This cataclysm is a force of natural events and is not within the scope of man to alter. Thus it must be regarded as a soul-cleansing process, for Divine laws are immutable, and when the shift arrives those who die will not be wiped out, but returned to spirit with opportunity for renewed spiritual growth. For this reason, we on this side are permitted to tell of the coming event, so that those in physical body will understand the principle and regard it in proper light. The passage from death to spirit, and spirit to physical life is one and the same process, no more to be feared than sleeping and wakening. Those who pass into spirit when the axis shifts will be free from pain and misery, while those who escape death will have an interesting time of it in restoring order and reviving the sweetness of spiritual knowledge. Archives will need to be buried deep in the earth so that future man will rediscover ancient truths and immortal written words. The destruction of libraries, art galleries, and laboratories will be enormous, but not all will be lost, and microfilming can preserve much knowledge.

Several shifts of the axis have occurred in ages past, raising mountains and destroying landmasses, and the one at the close of this century will be less catastrophic than the one that wiped out Lemuria, although great harm will be done to present structures and the way of life. Not all of that is bad, for certainly there is too much selfishness, sin, and crime, and much of this will be dissipated with the shifting, since men will be more afraid of the elements than of each other. Times of great peril draw man and beast together in common fear of the unknown, and this will prove true in the late nineties when this shifting occurs. Some lands will disappear under tons of water, while others will emerge and soon be ripe for cultivation. Outcroppings of older civilizations will appear, to the intense delight of surviving scholars. This shift is not to be dreaded, but simply prepared for through spiritual rebirth.

So many will die that zero population goals will be abandoned and family sizes increased to provide a work force for the future. This will bring men and women of all races closer together as they work in harmony to rebuild vestiges of societies. New waterways will be cut, and some old ones diverted to new pathways as the lands twist and tilt. Schools of the future will teach youngsters how to read portents and omens, as well as graphic arts and the printed word, and many will choose scientology as careers of the future.

Now let us speak of that awesome event. When the axis shifts it will seem to earthlings as if the sun has not moved across the heavens from horizon to horizon, although the sun will of course continue in its normal revolutions. We here already see this event occurring, so we understand the implications. It will be well for those there to understand that it is not the end of the world, but a process of readjusting sunshine and rain, the sea and the land, so that some areas of the earth are refreshed and others put out to pasture, so to speak. There will be some seas where there is now land, and vice versa, ice caps in new places, and balmy breezes at the poles. When the shift occurs, the souls then on earth will be terrified and turn to

God in their helpless fear, although some will unfortunately resume their nefarious ways. Yet on the embers of the devastated civilization will arise a better one based on brotherhood, and thereafter the return to earth of him who promised that when he came sinners would be separated from the near saints, and peace would reign for a thousand years. That time is not too far away, in the twenty-first century.

[Author's note: Because of this reference to the return of Jesus, I asked about Biblical predictions that the anti-Christ would come first. Their reply follows.]

The anti-Christ will be born within the next few years, and will be a threat to all when he grows to manhood. This is a real danger, for he will woo with silken voice and smooth manners, touting himself as the Messiah. He is so sure of a warm reception that he will enter the womb of a woman of means who is rather attractive, and is married to a fine man with position and talent. His birth will occur in the United States, and he will be dark-haired with blue eyes and a fair complexion. He will make his influence felt in 1995 or 1996, shortly before the shift of the axis, which he will survive and in fact profit by, since fear will grip the earth and he will allay those fears, saying that he is cleansing man of his wrongdoings and preparing for a better world. It is the opportunity for which he has long waited, but he will frighten and repel many who recognize the evil of his ways. Not all will succumb to his charms, and he will eventually be put to death.

Meteorites have peppered the earth in ages past, carving out vast bays and hollows, but except for a particularly heavy pelting at the time of Lemuria's demise, they have not tilted the earth from its assigned orbit. If a large meteorite is now in collision course with earth we do not see it here. Rather it will be the tinkering again with solar and nuclear forces, as well as volcanic eruptions that we see tilting the earth in the last of this century. Watch for a cooling trend shortly after the commencement of the eighties, and cyclones of increasing velocity that will herald the approaching shift. Some will talk of a new Ice Age, but it is actually the harbinger of the alteration of the earth's position in relation to the sun.

A race of people who suffered during the Hundred Years War is again being born into the earth plane, as we have said, in the hope of ending wars. They are peace-loving people, but so unsophisticated that the forward thrust of science will receive a setback in the first decades after century's end. Peace they will have, for their hatred of war tops all else, but they were pathetically undereducated during that hundred years of warfare, and have not applied themselves too diligently on the side where we are now. Thus so-called civilization will take a backward step while these simple people end wars by refusing to fight, but discoveries in technology and science have been racing ahead of man's ability to cope with the problems involved in using these discoveries. Thus it is necessary to step back and assimilate that which has been learned, before leaping ahead to more frightful advances. Man is lagging behind his machines. We have learned to win wars, but not to win the peace. Wars are an outrage against our Creator, who gave each of us the breath of life and the seed from which love springs. War has debased us all, whether we fight or profit from it, but these people now being born in increasing numbers will stop the warring between peoples who are, after all, a part of the one God and thus are brothers.

Those who fear death, whether from the shift of the axis or any other cause, should put it firmly from their minds. They fear the unknown, but they should realize that they are now in the actual unknown, whereas in many previous cycles they have been in spirit where we are now. Spirit is the normal pattern, whereas occupying flesh is an abrupt interruption of their spiritual being. If they contemplate the many risks they are now taking to meet karma and avoid amassing other karmic indebtedness each day of their lives, they will realize how truly brave they were to venture into the physical dimension. On this side where we are, the universal laws are such that we are relatively safe from temptations. Thus advancement is slower here, but also less risky in sliding backward from the goal of reunion with the Creator. We are in the natural form, spirit. You are in the abnormal form, for life began in our state, and we will eventually find eternal reunion from this state, so don't fear the transition termed death. It leads to normal being, free from handicaps and hurdles, and to eternal life.

Some religions teach of a heaven, a hell, and a purgatory. These are figures of speech for states of consciousness, because there is no place except *here,* where those in physical and spirit form intermingle. When we choose we can take on raiments and look just as we did when in the flesh, and it is then that we are sometimes glimpsed by earthlings who are able to describe our appearance. This is not usually an idle pastime, for it helps to establish the reality of continuing life. What we want to prove is that we are more alive here than in the flesh, because we are far more aware. The time will come before very long when those of you who wish to see us can develop mind pictures that will show on sensitive camera film, for we want you to know that we are available to comfort those in the difficult physical plane. Jesus of Nazareth comes and goes at will among those who need him or are in distress, for he is the perfect man who has free access to all seven planes, and to his Creator.

When man penetrates the mysteries of time and space he will have conquered the restraints of the flesh and be ready for higher development. This is all important to understanding Divine laws and the significance of one's own place in the universal plan. We here are unable to express it in terms you would understand, but it is there for the finding, and through meditation one will come to feel so much a part of the infinite that he will escape the confining restrictions of the physical body. Look then for a breakthrough in this field during the coming decade as science and medicine probe into inner man, and come to understand the importance of treating disease through ease and relaxation, for from our vantage point we see how the human species is tied in Gordian knots that restrict his mental and spiritual expansion. Relax, meditate, and feel a part of the whole of mankind, loving and blessing all that is good, and praying for destruction of that which is evil in man. This much we know: the two dimensions of spirit and physical being will become as one when universal law is more fully grasped. Feel the akinship with all of God's creations, and strive for that which is just. Banish fears, abolish angers, and work for the common good.

And on that solemn note, the Guides drew the curtain on the ancient past and the foreseeable future.

15

Afterthoughts

The Guides have become such comfortable friends during the past sixteen years of our collaboration that I sometimes appeal to them for answers to cosmic problems that are puzzling me. Since these same posers may have occurred to some of our readers. I will set them down in question-and-answer form:

Q. Is it true that praying over plants helps them to grow?

A. Since the beginning of earth time there has been a species of souls inhabiting forests, glens, and vales to tend the plants, trees, and flowers. They are elfin types who are not the same as human souls, but so similar as to seem like first cousins of homo sapiens. Their love for growing things encompasses the universe, and they dwell near them to guard them from harm. Mythology calls these beings elves, and that is not too far amiss, for they are little ones, when seen. Thus when you pray over a plant you are actually asking God to guard the little elf whose assignment it is to keep it growing, and these are friendly souls who want to associate with humans, so they strive to do their task even better when the plant is prayed over, wooed with music, or given particular attention. It is their task to encourage harmony within the universe, and when one prays over plants, or sings and talks to them, he is naturally contributing to harmonious surroundings and fulfilling the purpose of the particular little sprite who guards the plant.

Q. Is cremation or burial better for a human body?

A. No difference. The earth receives back its own, whether it be in the form of ashes or skin and bones, except that ashes are cleaner and require less space. To the soul it matters not.

Q. I have read that the soul lingers in the body for three days, and it is therefore better to delay cremation for that length of time. Is this true?

A. Nonsense. The soul withdraws at or before physical death, and what soul wants to hang around a shell that has been sluffed away? Some "attend" their funerals, but only to be around those they have known and loved.

Q. What do you think about artificially prolonging life with machines, after the brain is dead?

A. Not for us to decide.

Q. What about birth control, or abortions?

A. Anyone has a right to decide whether to bring another soul into being through her own body, but abortion is not the best means of preventing births, since it stops a marvelous process already begun, even though a soul has not yet entered the fetus. Better to use birth control.

Q. Why do you advise against eating the flesh of animals?

A. It makes one heavy, material, and earthbound. To achieve lightness and spirituality eat the fruits, berries, vegetables and nuts that abound on this planet. Eat lightly, but with well-balanced meals rich in carbohydrates and minerals as well as proteins from soybeans and other legumes. Notice the difference in the body and its odors. Red meat is especially bad, as it places one in the category of carnivorous animals and those who eat each other. Why laden the body with dead animals, when such a variety of healthful food avails?

Q. What of milk and cheese?

A. Perfectly all right, so long as it comes from contented cows who are glad to share their bounty and want to be hand-milked. In that event the vibrations are good, but not when mechanical milkers are used, because those are resented by cows accustomed to the loving touch of their keepers. Honey is an excellent food, as are fruits and fresh vegetables. Fish are as much a part of God's creation as we are, but like the plants they do not object to being eaten when taken painlessly and consumed with love. Some fowl may be eaten if taken joyfully for the essence, and not for the cruelty of hunting, but it is better to confine oneself to the fruits, nuts, and vegetables which give freely of themselves to fulfill their mission, which is the nurturing of others.

Q. What is the purpose of roaches, mosquitoes, and other annoying insects?

A. Roaches and other harmful forms of life, when in close contact with man, are not to be tolerated. They have their own sphere and are not to encroach on that of others. Although they too contain life, they will have to be exterminated whenever they have invaded the territory of man, for they are dangerous to health, as are flies when permitted to swarm about food that is to be eaten by man. These are some of the most ancient forms of life, carryovers from a vast prehistoric age, and rather than developing to higher states they have spent their time interfering with animals and humans until they are a plague on the planet. We do not foresee the outcome of this situation, but they should not be permitted life in the environs of man. As to the animals, also created before man, theirs was to have been a peaceful kingdom before God introduced homo sapiens. Under ideal conditions they could have coexisted pacifically, as once they did before man turned hunter, discovered how to make fire, and became aware than animal flesh was delicious when cooked. Thus although man was intended to thrive as herbivorous, he invaded the animal kingdom, and as he began to eat the flesh of this lower form of life, he took on animalistic traits of behavior. Best to return to peaceful coexistence and love the animals as little brothers, who although they lack our consciousness and growth potential, are beautiful and clean and friendly in their normal state of being.

Q. Is it sometimes wise to do nothing, in order to prevent the amassing of bad karma?

A. An oyster in its shell is incapable of wounding others, yet can itself be hurt when it emerges from that shell. So it is with people, who would do no wrong if we remained forever in our mother's womb, or drew ourselves into a shell of our own making and refused to venture forth. Granted? Yet it would be a total waste of all talents and opportunities for good, because unless we dare to venture forth on our own, sometimes even making serious mistakes, we cannot hope to complete the cycle of rebirths and rejoin the Creator. Thus it is better to sally forth and risk karmic entanglements in so doing, than to crawl into a shell and contribute nothing to others and to God. Do not fear to make mistakes or amass some karma, because in that same venture is the opportunity to do great good, and to benefit from the karmic influences that help us to grow and develop. Karma can be good as well as bad.

Q. Is it possible to reach God except as a Christian?

A. The one hope of human bengs is to find eternal reunion with their Creator, and for that reason it is unlikely that those who believe in other creeds will be denied the joy of that oneness. God's grace is not reserved alone for those fortunate enough to know about and believe in the divinity of Jesus Christ. Those of us who accepted and believed in Christ are fortunate to be well along the pathway toward an understanding of the Divine laws, yet we are but pilgrims, and like those of other faiths are required to cleanse our hearts of inferior thoughts and unkindnesses before rising higher toward this reunion with our Creator. Thus this is not a Christian heaven, but a way station en route to the higher realms, where we will learn how to worship God and express that adoration which is a part of Divine law.

Q. Why do you keep stressing that we should learn patience?

A. Patience is the art of the possible. When we expect more than we are capable of assimilating, we are pushing too fast in our soul's upward climb. Better to reach for a lamp than a star, if we are groping in the dark. Thus we achieve a goal that is available to our present state of development, and as each step is achieved we are ready for the next step on the upward climb. Patience is a matter of reaching for steady advancement, and if we push too hard we upset our glandular system, causing dissatisfaction, envy, and an assorted can of worms, for we paralyze our progress. In order to handle the steady climb we must set our goals within reachable limits, a little at a time, while we are steadily mounting. Humility is the art of grasping our own limitations, accepting the fact that we are mere specks in the galaxy of great beings, just as our earth is but a minor star in the firmament. Thus we say to ourselves, This you have accomplished, but look at the road ahead. Until you have completed the upward surge and are ready for reunion with the Creative Force, do not pause and congratulate yourself, for there is a long way yet to go.

Q. Will you explain how automatic writing works, and why I am sometimes a faulty transmitter?

A. Yes, we will discuss the problem of transmitting messages without coloration from the receiver's subconscious. What specifically occurs is that when one lets his mind or consciousness float free of entangling alliances with the physical body, the waves or vibrations interract with those entities of like pattern, so that the thinking or sending of messages here is caught by the one in flesh whose consciousness is temporarily floating free. It is an interception of rays or beams of thought which makes it possible for the receiver to sit at a desk or typewriter and transmit the motions of the spirit entity as if it were his own thoughts in a more conscious state. The subconscious automatically writes or types these thoughts or messages being transmitted, although the receiver is not necessarily in trance, as you are not. Nevertheless he has made himself susceptible to the wavelengths of others' thoughts to the extent that these impulses are automatically picked up by the subconscious and written or typed. The subconscious not only serves as a memory bank and storage file, but also as the weeder outer of bombardment from other planes as well as your own plane. What reaches the conscious mind is first strained through the subconscious, thus preventing a maze of conflicting material from jamming the conscious or operating level of the mind. It therefore affords a protection for one's privacy. When the subconscious ceases to serve as a screen, we say that a person is mad, hearing voices and seeing faces that are not there. Always preserve the subconscious as a shield between you and the world. But the day will come when all mankind will be able to communicate as freely with those of us on this side as with others in the flesh. The veil will be torn away, and all will realize that their time in the flesh is but a passing moment in the eternity of time. Those who need not return will help those in the flesh to advance rapidly and, in that time there will indeed be a kingdom on earth as well as in heaven, for in those last days the awareness of God will be so overwhelming that none would dare transgress his laws. We foresee this occurring in the not-too-distant future, but until then let us work toward awakening those who are failing to recall the wondrous theme of creation, exalting false gods, and preferring man-made pleasures to divinity.

Q. The medical profession is baffled by what it terms "crib deaths." Why does an apparently healthy baby go to sleep, never to reawaken, and autopsies reveal no cause of death?

A. Crib deaths occur when those who, having decided to enter physical body, feel that they had better reconsider earth life and withdraw before it is too late. Spirits deciding to reincarnate are given the right within a short period after physical rebirth to withdraw, if the circumstances have altered from those they had reason to expect would furnish a proper way to work out karma and advance spiritually. Sometimes it is a planned withdrawal in order to help a parent, through grief, learn a valuable lesson.

Q. What do you think about the death penalty?

A. The death penalty is a problem that will have to be faced, for when man defies his Creator by destroying in cold blood or hot anger the lives of others, he will have to be removed from the earth. It would seem from this side that no one who sins against God by taking lives he has created should be permitted to walk about endangering the lives of others. If a legally constituted body deems that the remainder of society is better off by removing one who is a danger to the citizenry, that person, having deliberately taken other lives, should of necessity relinquish his own, and after prolonged meditation on this side earn the right to another opportunity for penance in the flesh.

Q. What about outer-space beings and the UFOs?

A. Some are here on earth at all times, and others come and go, but they are definitely in contact with this planet. Do not think that because earthlings are not doing the same in outer space others are not here. Many UFO sightings are illusory or imaginary, but this is definitely a time of exploration, and because of changes already occurring in the earth, some are traveling here to see what it is all about. This is the important point: it will eventually be found that these souls from other planets are actually traveling instantaneously until they reach the outer areas of earth's gravitational and atmospheric pressures, at which time they assemble their vehicles from gaseous materials converted into solids. It sounds farfetched, but what we tell you is a fact that will soon be proven. These beings are not unlike earthlings except in their approach to cosmic problems, for their goals are vastly different than those of earthlings. They wish to speed up the process of reunion with God, whereas we here seem to want to prolong the luxury of earth living as if it were a goal itself, to prolong flesh rather than to become one with God. Thus we trail behind the more advanced planets in our primitive understanding of values, goals, and spiritual growth.

Q. Will the so-called "youthquake" subside, or become even more revolutionary?

A. The youth of the world will relax its tempestuous outbursts and become as youths once were in this country: disdainful of the older generations until they themselves join the workaday world and try to infuse it with bright new ideas. This revolt in which the earth is now engaged is engendered not by youth per se, remember, but by Atlanteans and the victims of recent wars who rushed back into flesh in rebellious mood. They are becoming adults, and the wave of violence and crime continues, but as these rebellious ones die out or are forced to face the facts of life they will become the middle-aged ones and less erratic. But remember, as long as these Atlanteans are here there will be some turmoil and unrest, for they are of that Atlantean period when ruling the world was their aim by fair means or foul. It will be a difficult time through the eighties and into the nineties, as we have told you. The so-called Third World is also peopled with these Atlanteans and those who met death in war through no fault of their own, and they also are flaming for revenge. As the world sows, so does it reap. After the turmoil, the shift of the axis will sweep away the mire of this twentieth century, the good as well as the evil. Not all of it, understand, but the earth will be making a rather fresh start in science, religion, and morals—see what we mean? Those remaining will have endured such a frightful natural disaster that they will be less willing to cause man-made disasters, and all will be pulling together for a time. Don't expect human nature to change overnight, however, because some will still be attempting to make personal gain out of disaster, while others will reach out for a clearer understanding of God. The situation will ease as it settles down to a new set of problems: feeding the survivors, avoiding radioactive gases, withstanding the elements, and superimposing good governmental structure atop the ashes of the present ones.

Q. Can you tell us more about the Second Coming?

A. As we have said, later in the twenty-first

century Jesus is planning to return to earth in a supreme try to restore God's kingdom here. The anti-Christ by then will have been slain, opening the way to the real Messiah, and as the earth has been swept clean through the frightful havoc wrought by the shift of the axis, so will men's hearts have been purified. Those living at the time of the Coming will be souls who have returned with a special mission to prepare the way for the Lord. As is always the case, not many will recall the pledge they made before returning to physical body, but enough will have progressed sufficiently through meditation and prayer to reawaken that memory; and when all is in readiness the Master will come again as a babe, to Mary. The earth's geography will be so altered that it is impossible for us to pinpoint the exact spot of his emergence from Mary's womb, although it seems to be in the Eastern Hemisphere. Some will ignore him as before, but many will be drawn as by a magnet to this exalted soul, who will step forward to lead men back to God and establish peace on this war-torn globe. We are permitted to say this now, in order to bring hope to bruised hearts and those who despair of any sort of spirituality in such a blasphemous place as earth is today.

Yes, earth will survive, and so will man, to be given yet another chance by a patient and loving Creator.